THE CHURCHES' FOLLY

Copyright 2008 by James Palmer

All rights reserved.

ISBN: 1439232636

EAN13: 9781439232637

Visit www.Createspace.com to order additional copies.

The Churches' Folly

False Assurance

James Palmer

DEDICATION

I want to acknowledge the help of my wife and son with their editing.

I dedicate this book to that beginning of our spiritual forefathers who endeavored to keep alive Biblical Christianity. Those who understood the urgency of Jude's admonition to *"earnestly contend for the faith that was once for all delivered to the saints."* They are to be seen in every age since the Apostles. Many paid with their lives for their efforts to obey Jude's instruction to the Lord's posterity. There have been so many on the Continent and Britain that space to enumerate will not be given. Suffering they did for the *light* they had and they tried to strengthen what remained of the Faith. But to name a few who saw a need of redress and pursued it, I trust in good faith, I cite George Calixus from 1260 A.D., who suggested that everything that came into the Church after the fifth Century should be thrown out; Martin Luther and Amino Simms who initially were trying to write some wrongs; Erasmus, who in his gentle and humorous way contributed to reform. Tyndale, Whitfield, Wesley, George Fox and so many more who in some way saw a need, sometimes imperfectly, but were however, willing to risk their lives for Reform needed and paid the price often they did.

From Britain and the Continent came these movements to the Americas'. The Salvationists who's Leader William Booth tried to reform the Church of England initially and would have stayed if they had not reneged on their Evangelism course. Methodism, the Nazarenes, Wesleyan, Assemblies, and a whole host of smaller Sects that had their roots in Holiness unto the Lord; yes, and to those individual Catholic Priests that had a heart for the truth and obeyed Pope John Paul II edict to preach holiness, I dedicate to their revival and renewed effort. To the old school Southern Baptist that has strayed, I exhort you to turn back to purity of life and stop trusting in your "stay out of hell pass" in "your sin gospel."

This Dedication is my heart! But the book's text is my zeal for the LORD and the Faith that was delivered from THE BEGINING ONCE FOR ALL. To you who find how far you have fallen I say on the Authority of the Lord himself, who has enabled me with His gift to charge you, **to be of one mind and one mouth** concerning the Gospel: (It may well cost you who heed the charge, your place or station), Dedicate yourself unto the Lord, not the teaching/traditions or commandments of men or a Sect, which so often are self-serving.

In reflecting on *such a cloud of martyrs* who counted *all things as loss* to achieve the *Excellency of Jesus Christ,* with longing and admiration I dedicate to their memory this *Contention* for their service to *the children of God.* If you are young in the Lord, this testimony is more than the *Milk of the Word,* chew slow and swallow slow, but do not fear the spirit of the message; you will be strengthened and established in understanding of God's Word. I dedicate this to such as you! As well, I dedicate this to the memory of my grandfather James Marvin Owen, who was ordained in 1910 to the society of the then Methodists. Also, to his youngest and now departed daughter, my mother. As with them, so with all who have and do love the Lord Jesus with all sincerity, I long for your fellowship even *as the whole Creation groans for the adoption.* And to all who long for His appearing I dedicate this book, *Even So, Come Lord Jesus.*

James Palmer

PREFACE

The personal side of this book arose from my search as to why so many Christian churches have a different point of view on Baptism. This became a wonderment to me because the Biblical writings seemed to contradict, at least in some manner, what was being taught in the churches today. I purposefully attended multiple denominations until I was satisfied I grasped their doctrinal views.

But having done so only fulfilled 1/3 of my chosen course of inquiry. Comparison of modern teaching with the Biblical record left a gap that needed to be filled by a source that was as close to the Apostles as could be found. That source was church history, and it was there that the differences in the churches teaching and the apostles' writings were made plain.

The fact that some churches hold Christian baptism to be just an ordinance and others teach it as a sacrament while others say it's irrelevant, only made my search and discovery more pertinent. These three views oppose one another, which make reconciliation of their teachings impossible. Because their gospels are basically the same, often thought not to be because of differing theological approaches, and is central to the disunity of Christian baptism's symbolism of purpose!

Baptism is listed in Acts chapter two as 1/3 of the Gospel. 1) *Repent,* 2) *be baptized,* 3) *you will receive the promised Holy Spirit.* (Number 3 has been argued amongst sectarians as to the Holy Spirit's proof of presence being spiritual *gifts* or spiritual *fruit* and has caused much neglect to occur with numbers one and two). While they all agree the first word of the Gospel is "repent", they are far from agreement that the second command is "be baptized: *for the remission of sin.*"

So it was the views, not the act or mode, of baptism that needed to be discovered in my search. And the early church's view and the apostles' teaching were discovered to be one and the same on baptism, through the first five centuries. Briefly, it is this: pre 431 A.D. Ephesus Council, the Universal Teaching was, *"no sin after baptism"*. Wow, who wants to hear that? Well, I stuck with it and discovered that even though *"the Way is straight and narrow"* that did not make the Way hard! As a matter of fact Jesus said, *"Take my yoke upon you and learn of me, for my yoke is easy and my burden is light"*.

It is their differences over the Baptismal Font that has *'bruised the gospel'* that I address in this book. You will be exposed to the declared truth of the past, and what it is claimed to be in the present. From there you will be able with a clear and *light* conscience decide your final course.

God speed.

INTRODUCTION

Calvinism, of course, originated with John Calvin. Well, not quite. It actually began with St. Augustine, the Bishop of Hippo, in the fifth century. Mr. Calvin picked up the tenets of *perseverance* and *irresistible grace* from Mr. Augustine. What follows is John MacArthur's teaching on Perseverance of the Saints. He is a conservative advocate of its tenets, as is the Westminster Catechism, often referred to as the Calvinist's Bible.

It has been said of truth that it goes through three stages. First, it is ridiculed. Second, it is violently opposed. Thirdly, it is accepted as self-evident. As you progress through the discourse that follows you will find yourself in one stage or the other. You will need to persevere through to the end of Mr. MacArthur's teaching of this subject for the reason that the evidence of contention becomes very clear as the discourse progresses. Certain facts that are often vigorously denied become self-evident. This often happens with much speaking, and this partial **Master's Seminary Journal** holds no exceptions to that rule. MacArthur's discourse below is from their teaching material and is presented by them as proof this is the Apostles' teaching.

PERSEVERANCE OF THE SAINTS
John F. MacArthur, Jr.
President and Professor of Pastoral Ministries

This message was published in The Master's Seminary Journal (TMSJ)
A copy of the Journal, and information concerning subscriptions can be obtained by writing:
The Master's Seminary Journal, 13248 Roscoe Blvd., Sun Valley, CA 91352
TMSJ 4/1 (Spring 1993) pp. 5-24

I have not changed one word in their Journal. I have, however, commented on it sufficiently to expose its errors and differences with the Scriptures. Emphasis has been added.

※ ※ ※

INTRODUCTORY NOTES

DEFINING TERMS

Dear Reader, a prerequisite to a clear understanding of the opposing views discussed in this book would be a clarification of the possible definitions of two words. Because there are differing views in Christendom on the meaning of these two important words, it is necessary to provide you with those differences. Having done so, you will be able to answer for yourselves, is there a provision in the Gospel, as delivered by the Apostles, to bring us into a walk of no sin? Experientially out of sin? To walk as Jesus walked (1Jn 2:6).

TWO VIEWS OF SIN

First, saint. In Strong's Concordance we find the word translated 'saint' as #40 in his Greek lexicon: *sacred* (physically *pure*, morally *blameless* or *religious*, ceremonially *consecrated*. In the Greek the literal translation for saint is a holy one. (The word translated 'holy' also being Strong's #40.) Liddell Scott Jones Greek-English Lexicon gives this definition: *devoted to the gods*; 1. in good sense, *sacred, holy* 2. of persons, *holy, pure*. The Oxford dictionary gives us: *a person acknowledged as holy or virtuous and typically regarded as being in heaven after death*.

    Second, sin. Strong's #G264: properly to *miss* the mark (and so *not share* in the prize), that is, (figuratively) to *err*, especially (morally) to *sin*. (That mark is the law. Romans 3:20)

    The 'legal' definition of sin used by those who hold to the assurances found in the Master's Seminary Journal by John MacArthur and Calvinists: **"To deviate in any manner from an absolute standard of perfect behavior."**

Now the 'ethical' definition of sin: **"To willfully transgress the known law of God."** Who's definition can we trust? There is a simple test that will reveal it. In the book *CONFLICTING CONCEPTS of HOLINESS*, by W.T. Purkiser, there are 37 verses, out of a total of 41, where the 'legal' definition will not fit. For purpose of space I will only list four.

> *1. In John 5:14, we read: "Afterwards Jesus findeth him in the temple, and said unto him, Behold, thou art made whole: sin no more, lest a worse thing come upon thee." Substituting the legal definition we would read: "Behold, thou art made whole:* **deviate no more in any manner from an absolute standard of perfect behavior,** *unless a worse thing come upon you." This would certainly place the poor fellow in a terrible spot! How could he avoid all deviations from a perfect standard, known or unknown, voluntary or involuntary? But when we insert the ethical definition of sin, our Lord's requirement becomes reasonable and, by God's grace, possible: "Behold, thou art made whole:* **willfully transgress no more the known law of God,** *lest a worse thing come upon you."*
>
> *2. Next test Romans 6:15: "What then? Shall we sin, because we are not under law, but under grace? God forbid." Substituting the legal definition we are confronted with this glaring absurdity: "What then? Shall we* **deviate in any manner from an absolute standard of perfect righteousness,** *because we are not under law, but under grace? God forbid." However, the ethical definition places before us the New Testament standard of Christian*

conduct: "*What then? Shall we* **willfully transgress the known law of God** *because we are not under law, but under grace? God forbid.*"

3. Next, is 1Cor 15:34: "*Awake to righteousness, and sin not; for some have not the knowledge of God: I speak this to your shame.*" *Inserting the legal definition, we would have,* "*Awake to righteousness, and never* **deviate in any manner from an absolute standard of perfect behavior;** *for some have not the knowledge of God.*" *Since those who hold this definition deny the possibility of living without sin in word, thought, and deed any day, this makes the verse an absurdity. However, the ethical definition reveals this as the universal obligation of all New Testament believers:* "*Awake to righteousness, and never* **willfully transgress a known law of God;** *for some have not the knowledge of God.*"

4. Lastly, 1 John 3:8-9, wherein two of the terms are nouns and two are verbs. However, the coherence of the passage demands that they be understood as bearing the same meaning. With the legal definition the verses would read: "*He who* **deviates in any manner from an absolute standard of perfect righteousness** *is of the devil; for the devil so* **deviates** *from the beginning..Whosoever is born of God does not* **deviate from absolute righteousness;** *for His seed remaineth in him; and he cannot* **so deviate**, *because he is born of God.*" *This would eliminate all finite human beings from the children of God,*

> *for sure! Now the ethical definition: "He who is* **willfully violating the known law of God** *is of the devil; for the devil* **so violates God's law** *from the beginning..Whosoever is born of God is not* **willfully violating God's known law;** *for His seed remaineth in him: and he cannot be* **willfully violating God's known law,** *because he is born of God."*

He cannot sin does not mean, he is not able to sin. Those who use the legal definition above often make this false assertion against those who proclaim the non-Calvinistic Gospel. **A sinning saint is an oxymoron.**

* * *

THIS IS A WORD FROM THE ALMIGHTY:

> *"Some love what they think My Word says,*
> *But they do not love the Truth.*
> *For when My Word speaks contrary to*
> *The doctrines and traditions of men*
> *They refuse My Word, which*
> *they profess to love."*

* * *

Narrow margin: Journal
Wide margin: Analysis

CHAPTER ONE

Peter's life exemplifies <u>what the doctrine of the perseverance of the saint's means in the life of</u> a faltering believer. Christ's present intercessory prayers assure that genuine believers will be saved to the uttermost. This is the doctrine of the perseverance of the saints.

A genuine believer is one that conforms to the image of God's Son in this life (Rom 8:29). A Calvinist contradicts this, as they teach a saint sins—*every day* in word, thought and deed (Westminster Catechism). The following verses address the claim that sin's corruption remains active in a Christian (Eph 4:13; Jn 8:31-35; Mat 5:8,48; Rom 8:2,4,29b; 2Tim 2:19; Heb 12:14; 1Pt 4:1; Rom 6:7,18). This discourse by John MacArthur will attempt to use Peter's early life to exemplify and confirm the falsehood of the sinning saint.

Those with true faith <u>will not lead perfect lives,</u>

What of Matthew 5:48? This is such a heresy to teach! The perfection Jesus taught in Matthew 5 is a moral perfection. It is stated as an imperative, which means it is *mandatory*, not optional or positional as the Calvinist teaches, (Mat 5:48; Rom 12:2; 2Cor 12:9 ESV; Php 3:15; Col 3:14; Heb 5:9, 12-14, 6:1,11:40,12:23; Jam 1:4, 3:2; 1Jn 4:18). Christian perfection and holiness is how the saint is made known. The immoral, willfully sinning professing Christian is defiled and needs to obey the first word of the gospel—repent. Not, as Peter says, like a dog *'who goes back to its vomit'*; rather as Matthew 1:21 and Luke 1:75 say, *"in true righteousness and holiness before Him all the days of our lives"*. The Calvinist insists this is 'positional'. Could true holiness and righteousness be positional?

> *though some have attributed such a claim to proponents of working-faith salvation. The teaching of "once saved, always saved" may carry the false implication that after "accepting Christ" a person may live any kind of life and still be saved. That leaves out the doctrine of perseverance, which carries with it the need for a holy life.*

Does this mean he believes a Christian cannot be perfect, but they need to be holy? This is what George Orwell called 'doublespeak'. It will be repeated often, stay tuned.

> *Peter in his first epistle furnishes six means through which God causes every Christian to persevere: by regenerating them to a living hope, by keeping them through His power, by strengthening them through tests of faith, by preserving them for ultimate glory, by motivating them with love for the Savior, and by saving them through a working faith.*

> *Quantification of how much failure the doctrine of perseverance allows is impossible, but Jesus did prescribe a way for the church to deal with a professing believer whose life sin had seemingly come to dominate.*

This claim by Mr. Murray with John MacArthur's agreement is a direct contradiction of every address Jesus made on sin. They assert the claimed virtue of *Perseverance* over *Once Saved Always Saved* to be the need for a holy life, and then deny that necessity can be met by hiding it under the assumed idea that quantification of how much failure perseverance provides for is impossible. This is a plain promotion of unholiness. Peter shows how to *quantify* how much failure. That quantification is a big zero! "Therefore, brothers, be all the more diligent to make your calling and election sure, for if you practice these qualities you will **never** fall". 2Pt 1:10

Do they or he ever admit this place in the Gospel? Not that I can find. Therefore, I call them *heretics* and *apostates*. They have departed from the truth, or having not come to it yet, deny it exists! Those who point out what the Word really teaches are referred to as Pharisees, self-righteous, believers in John Wayne Christianity, teachers of works righteousness or stiff shirts.

> *"In order to place the doctrine of perseverance in proper light we need to know what it is not. It does not mean that every one who professes faith in Christ and who is accepted as a believer in the fellowship of the saints is secure for eternity and may entertain the assurance of eternal salvation. Our Lord himself warned his followers in the days of his flesh when he said to those Jews who believed on him, "If ye continue in my word, then are ye truly my*

> *disciples, and ye shall know the truth, and the truth shall make you free" (John 8:31,32).*

Herein lies great deception. Mr. MacArthur suggests that truth sets free, but does not finish the context of that truth, which is free **from sin;** the very truth that provides the condition of *remaining in the house forever.* He again, in this fashion, makes truth arbitrary. This Jesus did not do, but the Calvinist does. (See John 8:31-35, *the complete context.*)

> *He set up a criterion by which true disciples might be distinguished, and that criterion is continuance in Jesus' Word."*

That Word says *'free from sin'.* A real possibility *all the days of our lives,* contrary to Calvinism that denies this rule.

> *The above explanation by Murray of the doctrine of perseverance is an elaboration of what Peter meant by his words "protected by the power of God" when he wrote his first epistle (1Pet 1:5). If any biblical character was ever prone to failure, it was Simon Peter.*

The above explanation by Murray, a Calvinist, is not an elaboration of what Peter meant, but of what they *mean* Peter to be saying. The grace of God is what protects us because it is given to us to be strong in the Lord and the power of His might. Plus, 1Peter 1:5 says this power to be kept comes *through faith.* Because they change the meaning of grace to mercy, in most cases, it leaves them kept *in sin* to one degree or another. This is another gospel. See Romans 5:21.

When Peter wrote his epistle he had already been converted, meaning he was now empowered with the Spirit of Holiness (Lk 22:32). You and I are commanded to walk in that Spirit of Power, which will provide for *all the righteous requirements of the law to be fully met in us,* Romans 8:4, the very thing that accomplishes Luke 1:75 in our lives.

> *Judging from the biblical record, none of the Lord's disciples 'excluding Judas the betrayer' stumbled more often or more miserably than he.*

While the record shows Peter to have sinned before he was converted, and this while being an apostle, we only have one example given of Peter being in the wrong after Pentecost, where the promised Holy Spirit was given for power. This was regarding him being afraid of men, when he acted *"contrary to the gospel"* concerning the Gentiles while with the disciples of James. This fear of men in regards to the truth of the gospel many of you possess! How so? For the sake of men's approval you will not go outside the camp and suffer with Jesus. That was the issue and Paul revealed it to him. While it is clear from the account that Peter was in the wrong, (as Paul declared *"I withstood him to his face"*, Gal 2:11), it does not with any certainty follow that this *partiality* in fear of the Jews on Peter's, or Barnabas', part was a *"willful sin"*. The Greek declares it to be *"less than walking in a straight line"*; therefore it could just as easily be called *an imperfection* as opposed to a *sin*. Sin we are commanded to stop in 1Corinthians 15:34. Perfection we are told to "go on to" in Hebrews 6:1. Holiness and perfection are not synonymous. The one is expected of us now, the other to pursue hotly.

※ ※ ※

CHAPTER TWO

Peter was the disciple with the foot-shaped mouth. He seemed to have a knack for saying the worst possible thing at the most inappropriate time. He was impetuous, erratic, vacillating sometimes cowardly, sometimes weak, sometimes hotheaded. On several occasions he merited strong rebukes from the Lord, none more severe than that recorded in Matt 16:23: "Get behind Me, Satan! You are a stumbling block to Me; for you are not setting your mind on God's interests, but man's." That occurred almost immediately after the high point in Peter's experience with Christ, when Peter confessed, "Thou art the Christ, the Son of the living God" (Matt 16:16).

This only proves the need to go on to perfection, (2Cor 7:1 and Heb 6:1), the very thing we are all told to do, and Peter did! Do you suppose him to have been a hypocrite? Many do. (As they do Paul, by insisting his **saying**, "I am the chief of sinners", meant he was in active, willful sin after his conversion.) Here is exactly where John Calvin, a Catholic, and John MacArthur, a Protestant, miss the mark, as do most Evangelicals, with their 'sinning saint' tradition. Moral perfection defines a saint. Conversely, Calvinism and the Westminster Catechism, as well as their non-Reformed counterparts, provide a go to heaven anyway 'gospel'. They do this by defining sin contrary to Romans 3:20.

Once they established their false definition of sin it was then easy for the devil, through these false ministers, to infect the churches with a standard called 'the sinning-saint'. Having defined sin as a *"deviation from an absolutely perfect standard of righteousness, known or unknown"*, the bar now being set beyond God's standard, the hope of not sinning is established out of reach! Legitimately defined sin having lost its place, the unholy believer is established. You see, to really persevere as a saint we must *'keep ourselves from sinning, so the Evil one does not touch us'* (1Jn 5:18). This verse a Calvinist will typically deny and, instead, run to chapter one verse eight. I will fully address that verse later on in this exposé of Perseverance.

> *Peter's life is proof that a true believer's spiritual experience is <u>often filled with ups and downs</u> but Peter illustrates another biblical truth, a more significant one: the keeping power of God. On the night Jesus was betrayed, He gave Peter an insight into the behind-the-scenes spiritual battle over Peter's soul: "Simon, Simon, behold, Satan has demanded permission to sift you like wheat; but I have prayed for you, that your faith may not fail" (Luke 22:31-32, emphasis added).*

Again, all this was before Peter's conversion and Holy Spirit filling, a fact not mentioned by Mr. MacArthur. I wonder why. The <u>often filled with ups and downs</u> is plainly to promote the *heresy* of 'the often sinning saint'. This is minimized by the phrase 'ups and downs', deceptive words. Make no mistake about it, MacArthur is not talking about emotional ups and downs but often filled bouts of sinning.

> *Peter was confident of his willingness to stand with Jesus, whatever the cost. He told the Lord, "Lord, with You I am ready to go both to prison and to death" (Luke 22:33). Yet Jesus knew the truth and sadly told Peter, "The cock will not crow today until you have denied three times that you know Me" (Luke 22:34).*

And this means we can and will sin like this after our conversion? Mr. MacArthur wants Peter to appear to be permanently erratic, vacillating, cowardly, weak, and hotheaded to promote his contention it is a normal Christian life. This is the devil's work that Jesus came to destroy (1Jn 3:8). On top of this, he insists a Christian cannot expect 'full and final salvation' from sin till Second Advent. Calvinism is one of the Serpents tools to perpetuate his work of sin. Did you read 1John 3:8? Jesus told the Jews they were the devils children because they did his will, (John 8:44). It is applicable to false teachers today who call themselves Christians. This is a serious charge, but must be made on the basis of their denial of present-tense holiness and teaching against Christian perfection defining sainthood.

> *Did Peter fail? Yes, miserably. Was his faith overthrown? Never. Jesus Himself was interceding on Peter's behalf, and His prayers did not go unanswered.*

This is to teach that a faith that holds on to the notion of eternal life, while in sin, is the answer to Jesus' prayer. Freedom from sin is why Jesus came. It was not without effect on Peter. Many are and have been "miserable, poor, blind and naked", but Jesus says 'if you will turn I will restore you'. Peter did. 'If you will submit to Him' He will not "blot your name from the Book of Life". Peter submitted. Peter turned from his ignorance and Jesus restored him and he obeyed the *holy commandment* thereafter. How are you doing? Peter meant well, but he needed conversion 'to all things new'. He got there with the Lord's help and the same Lord will give the same help to us, on the basis of the *'words of God falling on good ground'*. But if our hearts are not prepared to receive the "engrafted Word", we are admonished to *"break up our fallow ground"* so the Word can take root and not be taken away by the Evil one or the cares of this life (Jer 4:3; Hos 10:12). This is the purpose of this book. A confession of faith that anybody can make or claim is not the same as *'the answer of a good conscience before God'*. Oh, how men can convolute the Lord's teaching and still call it the 'restored' gospel when it *"is no gospel at all"*

※ ※ ※

CHAPTER THREE

The Lord intercedes for all genuine believers that way. John 17:11 gives a glimpse of how He prays for them: "I am no more in the world; and yet they themselves are in the world, and I come to Thee. Holy Father, keep them in Thy name, the name which Thou has given Me, that they may be one, even as We are" (emphasis added)

But who among them really believes it? This prayer speaks of Union. *Conforming to the image of God's Son,* (Rom 8:29), is the end to which Jesus was praying and the apostle taught. It is the fulfillment of this prayer, while we live in the flesh, which enables Jesus to come back *'for a bride without spot, wrinkle or any such thing'.* This is not 'Perfection of Oneness by Second Advent', but oneness of and by *obeying Jesus.* As He said, *"it is enough for the servant to be as his Master".* He did not mean we are to be so after death or at His appearing only, but now and *"unto the end".* 1Corinthians 1:8, *He will also keep you firm to the end, so that you will be faultless on the Day of our Lord Jesus Christ.* Do I hear any Calvinists saying amen?

> *He continues:*
> *I do not ask Thee to take them out of the world, but* to *keep them from the evil one.*

According to 1John 5:18, God has answered that prayer! How? Look and see.

> *They are not of the world, even as I am not of the world. Sanctify them in the truth; Thy word is truth.*

How were they to be sanctified? *"Doing no sin"* is continuing in Jesus' teaching, which *truth makes us free* (Jn 8:31-35). If we find ourselves in sin it is because we are not abiding in the Truth. Peter tells us *'the divine nature'* has been granted for us now, and states which *'qualities'* we are to add to our character, *'through God's divine power and promises'*, and that doing so will cause us *'to never fall'* (2Peter 1:1-10). It is not because we are persevering in our *'fallen nature'* while waiting for His appearing. Deny it all they like, it is exactly what they are teaching. *This is the will of God for you, even your sanctification.* Persevering *by abiding in these things*, not in iniquity. This establishes the doctrine, the purpose and the means of *"no sin after baptism"*. The apostasy of the 'sinning-saint' teaching, (yea, its promotion), makes its adherents "heretics" and "self condemned" and "sinning", (Titus 3:10-11).

    Christian Baptism, as an Apostolic Rite, is mandatory to eternal life because it is reckoned as the death of the sin nature and is symbolic of putting your sins away from you. This is the Christian's public confession of death to the bondage of sin and rising a servant of righteousness! This baptism is a witness to the death of the sin nature, which puts sin in

n. Once embraced heart, mind, strength and soul, ...es an *easy burden and a light load*. The *narrowness* ...aightness of this *Way* is the hard part. Sin, on the ...and is indeed bondage and heaviness of spirit that ...rd bids us cast on Him. To neglect this invitation is to ...death!

> *As Thou didst send Me into the world, I also have sent them into the world. And for their sakes I sanctify Myself, that they themselves also may be sanctified in the truth. I do not ask in behalf of these alone, but for those also who believe in Me through their word; that they may all be one even as Thou, Father, art in Me, and I in Thee, that they also may be in us; that the world may believe that Thou didst send Me.*

Sanctified in the truth. So then, how is *sanctification* prevented? By being out of the truth! Is this why Calvinism leaves *sanctification unfinished* until "Christ's appearing"? The answer is an unavoidable affirmative. The truth is there is no sanctification for those abiding in falsehood! "*Self imposed worship and harsh treatment of the body does not eliminate the sinful desires of the fallen nature. It only succeeds in false humility,*" which will not manifest the 'Spirit of sanctification,' instead just a 'religious spirit.' But what does 'eliminate the sinful desires of the fallen nature' is identifying with Christ's death to sin. Calvinism renders Christ's sacrifice impotent, by making it only a covering for sin and not a purification of the acts of sin as well. Their false claim that they teach purification now, is denied by their assertion the Christian, like the Apostle, will only finally 'cease from the propensity to sins' at Christ's appearing, (when there will be no more sin to overcome). How convenient for them.

> *And the glory which Thou has given Me I have given to them; that they may be one, just as We are one; I in them, and Thou in Me, that they may be <u>perfected in unity</u> that the <u>world may know that Thou didst send Me</u>, and didst love them, even as Thou didst love Me (John 17:15-23, emphasis added).*

Well, 'perfected in unity' is certainly part of Jesus' prayer and the provision for it to be granted by the Father provided in Ephesians 4:11-13. Is this fulfillment reserved only for Christ's appearing as well? Was the Father only able to answer Jesus' prayer in part? Without a teaching that states "no holiness no heaven" and that this holiness, just as unity, is for all the days of our lives, we are left with empty promises and Jesus' prayer unanswered till an indefinite time. (A time called "the article of death", or a time the Dispensationalists say happens in a Jewish Kingdom they call the Millennium.) This would make His departing prayer pointless, discredit the very early Church's unity and the historical record of Polycarp who said, "We do no sin here!" Just as the Lord commands and as the Apostles' gospel teaches. 'sin no more' obeyed. Could *"that the world may believe and know..."* be reserved for Second Advent?

> *Notice what the Lord was praying for: that believers would be kept from the <u>power of evil</u>; that <u>they would be sanctified by the Word</u>; that they <u>would share His sanctification and glory</u>; and that they <u>would be perfected in their union with Christ and one another</u>. He was praying that they would persevere in the faith.*

"Error, indeed, is never set forth in its naked deformity, lest, being thus exposed, it should at once be detected. But it is craftily decked out in an attractive dress, so as, by its *outward form, to make it appear to the inexperienced more true than the truth itself"*. (Irenaeus)

Share Jesus' sanctification and perfected union when? Now or in heaven? If not till heaven then they become part of glorification only. If here, as Jesus was here, then the prayer was meant to be answered here! Yes, persevere in a faith that really teaches union, which entails believing, and thereby, obeying the command of true holiness all the days of our lives. That is the truth that Mr. MacArthur comes near to, but denies! Jesus said that *truth would set you free from sin.* He did not say that truth would 'almost' set you free. Truth is absolute, not arbitrary. The last statement of MacArthur above, "He was praying that they would persevere in the faith" is true! Unfortunately MacArthur and Calvinists contend it is only to be partial for now, not a sanctification and unity that will be *"all the days of our lives"* (Lk 1:75). This will become more apparent as you progress in his discourse presented in this book.

> *Was the Lord praying for the eleven faithful disciples only? No. He explicitly includes every believer in all succeeding generations: "I do not ask in behalf of these alone, but for those also who believe in Me through their word" (v.20). That includes all true Christians, even in the present day!*

Amen! This means the *"will of God for us in Christ Jesus is our sanctification"*. Union is doing the Father's will, always, as Jesus did. Do Calvinists really teach this happens to, (as MacArthur calls them), "true" Christians all the days of their life? Again, herein lies the heresy of the Reformed Faith, it never really reformed.

I was doing one on one visitation with pastors of various churches to discuss and promote the real Gospel. A pastor said, "The Bible says we can sin." I replied, "Indeed it does and it also says we may *not* sin." His countenance fell, (as many others have), and he was then angry with me as I added, "Why then do you put the back seat in the front and the front seat in the back?" The interview was over at that point. Proving the phases of the truth: *ridiculed, violently opposed or accepted as self-evident.* I do recall a Disciples of Christ Church pastor receiving the message well and inviting me back.

> *Moreover, the Lord Himself is continuing His intercessory ministry for believers right now. "He is able to save forever those who draw near to God through Him, since He always lives to make intercession for them" (Heb 7:25). The King James Version translates Heb 7:25 thus: "He is able also to save them to the uttermost that come unto God by him, seeing he ever liveth to make intercession for them" (emphasis added).*

SAVED TO THE UTTERMOST

> *All true believers will be saved to the uttermost. Christ's High Priestly ministry guarantees it.*

Ah, *to the uttermost* indeed. Do you, reader, believe it? It means you really can be set free from sin. Do you want it? *To the uttermost* can be yours. The WORD declares it, (Rom 6:18, 8:2; 2Cor 6:17-7:1; Lk 1:75). "He is able..." Hebrews 7:25, indicates that we can come before the Throne of Grace to receive help before we fall, (1Cor 10:13), because He is always available for those *who draw near to God through Him.* Help before we endeavor in our own power and fail! Hebrews 4:15-16 speaks of seeking Him because of our "infirmities", which is different than waiting until those weaknesses bring us into actual sin, which is a "fall". Hebrews 7:25 and 4:15-16 tell us He is a faithful high priest, <u>guaranteed</u> to be available to intercede with the Father when we draw near to God. Not the guarantee suggested by Mr. MacArthur. God's conditions are required. (The Catholic and Protestant take on Heb 7:25 is one of their basis for the "confessing in sin", which has distracted from "salvation from sin".) This is putting *'a dress on error to make it appear to be more truthful than truth.'*

The Reformed Churches have a partial salvation in this life, to the uttermost at His appearing only. This means *no sanctification till the end.* Their gospel teaches saved *in* your sins and it is a 'lie from the Pit'. Matthew 1:21, says *away from* (Strong's #575), your sin, which leaves sinlessness. Matthew 1:21 says, '.you will call his name Jesus for he will save/deliver his people *away from their sin.* This is very clearly not **in** sin. Nor does it say deliver away from *the guilt and consequences.* Calvinists by this mean saved from hell, not acts of sin. However, their Catechism contradicts the scripture at this juncture, because "away from *their* sins" is personal and a true deliverance; as opposed to the corporate *guilt* idea that leaves 'personal' sin at least partially intact.

Compared with Luke 1:75 we have, without the remotest doubt, a Savior who came to deliver us *to the uttermost* from all acts, transgressions, practice, propensity, bondage, attachment, power, dominion, and violations of the righteous requirements of God's law, which the Holy Spirit defined as sin (Rom 3:20). His intent and power is sufficient to save you and me *away from* all these, not only of our "past" sins, but keep us from *"every act"* that leads to death (Heb 9:14)! This is the Good News called the Gospel! There is no other! Those who teach there is are Anathema, so decreed the Apostle. Calvinism and its Perseverance doctrine is a saved in your sin gospel that is no gospel at all! Great darkness covers the land, yes, and the world.

They have been justified,

It is here that the Evangelical makes an unbiblical claim, they teach a *carte blanche* justification for all sin, *past, present and future*. The Scripture states no such a thing, but it does proclaim justification for all **"past" sins,** (Rom 3:25; Heb 9:15; 2Pt 1:9). Any present sin may or may not be forgiven, depending on three factors: 1) *repentance,* 2) *"sins of ignorance",* 3) that spoken of in Hebrews 10:26, *"willfully sinning after coming to a full knowledge of the truth."* That same truth Jesus said would 'set us free from sin' (Jn 8:31-35). Freedom in the here and now that certain teachers won't admit to directly, but hide behind words and innuendos to make you think they do. *All liars* will be where? (Rev 22:15)

'they' are being sanctified

Operative word: being. To a Calvinist, are being sanctified means individual sanctification is a continuing process never finished until death or Jesus' appearing. A popular gospel widely held in Protestantism; in Catholicism it is finished in Purgatory. In the verses that follow sanctified is always in the present or past tenses. Act 20:32, 26:18, Rom 15:16, 1Co 1:2, 6:11, 7:14, 1Ti 4:5, 2Ti 2:21, Heb 2:11, 10:10, 10:14, 10:29, Jud 1:1.

The word 'being', as in Hebrews 10:14, is applied to the ongoing process of new believers entering into Christ, not as Mr. MacArthur is teaching, as an ongoing work in 'true' Christians. Once conversion is entered into, as with Peter, *"sin must cease".* This is the true definition of present tense sanctification, which MacArthur and Calvinism will not acknowledge. Biblical salvation is said to be *Today." today if you hear his voice, harden not your hearts"* as in the Provocation, (where they tried and tested God for 40 years). This is exactly what today's churches are doing with their erroneous teaching on sanctification. It is a provocation to our Holy God to disobey the command and not be holy for a lifetime; trusting in a justification of present sins that is only stated to be for sins that are **"past."**

In all the verses that mention an inheritance for *'those having been sanctified'* the tense is Greek perfect, which means they **were** sanctified and have remained in it! This is why sanctification precedes justification as in 1Corinthians 6:11. That is why Church Father's like John Chrysostom used the phrase, "maintaining your baptism."

Therefore, it is misleading to use the verse that refers to 'they' and apply it to the singular individual that has already entered Christ. All that are 'in Christ' are sanctified because that means their sins are in remission. 'They', referred to by MacArthur, are not sanctified because they haven't died to their sin yet and so are not even in Christ, because *'in Him is no sin'*. If they are not sanctified, they are not justified (1Cor 6:11). If they are not justified their past sins are still present sins, and they are dead while they live. If presently in your sins you have not obeyed the Lord's command to *"sin no more"*, and thusly, Christ is not your Savior! If they haven't kept Jesus' command they do not love Him, nor do they **"believe into Him".** They are not sanctified, because we are "sanctified through faith" (Acts 26:18).

Properly, what exists in so many churches are religious people who really are just "inquirers" or "learners". They are in church, even for years, yet have never obeyed the Lord's *holy commandment*! I do not fault them per-se because they haven't been taught the Faith because the clergy can't teach what they don't, or won't, believe. And the denominational leaders that used to believe being a Christian meant a sanctified believer, simply 'wandered away from the truth' for the same reasons they did in 431 A.D., to appease the people so that they don't lose members. If it had remained profitable to continue teaching the real gospel they would have; it wasn't, so the bar was lowered. The arrogance of the Magistrium, who labor for their superiors' teachings and rules, are not the Lord's ministers but man's! Lawlessness is sin. *'Love for God and neighbor will take you far from all sin'* (Polycarp).

> *and they will be glorified. Not one of them will miss out on any stage of the process, though in this life they all find themselves at different points along the way. The truth has been known <u>historically as the perseverance of the saints.</u>*

Historically, if you believe truth and history began with the Reformation. The apostles' and very early Church writings confirm a mandatory cessation of sin. In fact, Paul and Peter taught it was at Baptism this was to be obeyed. John Chrysostom taught that what Paul was teaching in Romans 7:14-8:29, was a complete deliverance from sin, in this life and time, all our days, as does Luke 1:75. *Moreover whom he did predestinate, them he also called: and whom he called, them he also justified: and whom he justified, them he also glorified* (Rom 8:30). Predestinate, called, justified, glorified are all in the past tense! How can this be seeing I would know if I were glorified? The point is, God knows! In other words, *'predestinated according to God's foreknowledge'* does not mean He decided you would be sanctified and your neighbor wouldn't. Calvinism teaches it this way and it is false! But because they do, they can then assume perseverance means a **guaranteed inheritance** for a sinning confessor of Jesus, who they call a saint. The site below records John Chrysostom's Homily on Paul's teaching of baptism and Paul as Saul being under the law and sin, and what Romans 8:2 accomplishes in a believer's life.

The Reformation did not take Christianity back to its roots at all! It primarily just left Papal rule behind. It did not reinstate 'perseverance of the saints', as that doctrine did not exist until John Calvin. The phrase would be accurate enough if it taught perseverance from sin to eternal life, for that is what the Word teaches in Romans 2:5-8 and chapter six.

www.ccel.org/fathers2/NPNF1-11/npnf1-11-77.htm#TopOfPage Homily XI on Rom. vi. 5. Homily XIII on Rom. vii.14

(The Links above are to Wheaton College, which is a Calvinistic School. Their side notes can be misleading)

* * *

CHAPTER FOUR

No doctrine has been more savaged by the system of theology that advocates merely intellectual faith as the condition of salvation, because the doctrine of perseverance is antithetical to the entire system that is so oriented.

Amen, but lordship salvation teachers like MacArthur do little better!

In fact, what proponents of this system have pejoratively labeled "lordship salvation" is nothing other than the doctrine of perseverance! Perseverance means that "those who have true faith can lose that faith neither totally nor finally."

New Testament faith is faith in God. Every person has faith in something, but *'not all men have faith in God'*. There is little faith, there is great faith, and you can pretend to have faith in God, which is *"feigned faith"*. Calvinistic trickery insinuates that all failed faith was untrue to begin with!

There is no such thing as true or false faith! Faith is still faith, even if in something false. True Faith is a term made up by MacArthur! Paul notes a first faith that they 'cast off'. (1Ti 5:12) ... **having damnation, because they have cast off their first faith.** Paul says faith can be cast off, which proclaims it to have been faith that was indeed true, otherwise damnation would not have been the result of it being cast off! MacArthur states those who have faith cannot lose that faith! Casting it off is very much a loss of faith. According to MacArthur, a beginning faith would have to not be true faith. Paul did not call this referenced faith *a feigned faith*, but faith! It was always faith through which Paul's subject, (and we), are saved IF we do not depart from it. *'If we deny Him, He will remain faithful to Himself'* for *'He cannot deny Himself'*. Keeping faith means remaining faithful to the Faith (Lk 9:23; 2Tim 2:13).

An argument by numerous Calvinists that Jesus, having used the phrase *"I have lost not one..."* meant you can lose your faith neither totally or finally. They believe this to be so from a misapplication of the two scriptures quoted below, wherein Jesus states a fact about those who had been with Him from the *'beginning only'*, (Jn 15:27). This does not extend to us.

BEHOLD:

While I was with them in the world, I kept them in Your name; I guarded those whom You gave to Me, and not one of them was lost, except the son of perdition, that the Scripture might be fulfilled. (Jn 17:12)

"Jesus answered, I told you that I AM; then if you seek me, allow these to depart", (that the Word might be fulfilled which He said, "Of those whom You gave to Me, I lost not one of them.") (Jn 18:8-9)

Another proof of this misapplication is the record of a large number of disciples *"turning back and walking with*

Jesus and the Twelve no more" (Jn 6:66). And it was to the *beginning disciples* only that Jesus' prayer in regards to *"losing none"* was and is applicable. Read John 15:27-17:12 and you will see it is one discourse with the same audience. Sorry, that's just the way it is.

Look, it is a comfort to think this is applicable to all who imagine a saint is kept in their sin and cannot be lost. The verses above state the disciples were kept by Jesus *while He was in the world!* 'Kept them while in this world' could not mean from hell, unless you think hell is in this world? Watched over/kept/guarded is not the same as 'saved'.

The Word now tells us to keep *ourselves* from sin, through faith, by the power of God. The responsibility of maintaining our faith is ours. The responsibility of supplying the power (grace) is His. As far as our life, that is our physical selves, Jesus kept their lives while with them on this earth. Yes, you could even include their souls in the keeping. But to teach this means a guarantee of eternal life for them all, or Peter as Mr. MacArthur states, is contradicted by Jesus Himself in Luke 12:46 where Peter is told, *"If you are not doing what I commanded you when I return I will cut you asunder and appoint your place with the unbelievers"*.

What I claim above agrees with Jesus' threat to Peter, and also to the Gentile believers in Revelation 3:5, where the unfaithful, (those not doing what Jesus commanded them), who did not repent, would be blotted out of The Book of Life. If their understanding of the perseverance of the saints were true there would be no need for such a threat at all, because as Mr. MacArthur and all Calvinists contend, *"it is Jesus who will keep us"*. If that were so, there would be no danger! God does not make idle threats. So seeing there is such a danger of rejection for those who do sin, (Mat 7:23), it becomes apparent that *WE* must *"keep ourselves from sin"* (1Jn 5:18), doing so by the grace of God that saves us through a faith that produces obedience to be holy (2Pt 1:3-4). As stated before faith is faith, even if in something false, even if it is in Calvinistic Perseverance of the Saints or a Baptist Eternal Security or the Vineyard's Once Saved Always Saved. Unfortunately, faith in something false neither makes the false thing true or the true thing false!

Faith in a faith that cannot be lost makes my faith in this claimed faith the very thing that guarantees I will be saved! This is Calvinism's, (and Evangelicalism's), circular reasoning! This is not how we are saved "through faith", rather God's grace is the vehicle of victory and our abiding in that victory is our faith that "overcomes the world." This is how we are saved to the uttermost! Faith in God, who has made available the power for us to become His sons and daughters, is not acquired through a belief in a system that leaves you to operate in the fallen nature! That is why they do not profess the completeness of God's salvation from sin's acts and dominance until Christ's appearing.

> *It echoes God's promise through Jeremiah: "I will make an everlasting covenant with them that I will not turn away from them, to do them good; and I will put the fear of Me in their hearts so that they will not turn away from Me" (32:40, emphasis added).*
>
> *That flatly contradicts the notion entertained by some who teach that faith can evaporate, leaving "believers" who no longer believe.*

Says Mr. MacArthur and Calvinists and Evangelicals in general! First of all, to believe is to obey, therefore 'willful disobedience is a departure of faith'. Concerning faith not evaporating, understand this: Heb 11:8, "By faith Abraham obeyed"; Heb 11:20 "By faith Isaac blessed." Heb 11:24 "By faith Moses refused..." Heb 11:29 "By faith the people crossed the Red Sea"... But they would not venture into giant territory because their faith evaporated.

When Messiah came, whom they believed would come, as a covenant people their faith was in a different kind of Messiah. (Just as many believe God's salvation today to be different than it really is.) Their faith was in something false. Therefore, they would not obey Him and the kingdom was taken from them and given to a nation that would produce its fruit, (Mat 21:43). They ceased to be the people of God, just as King Saul of old who was rejected because he did not obey the word of the LORD. (MacArthur claims God's warnings do not negate His promises!) This cost them the Kingdom! And unbelief displayed in a non-sanctified life, if not repented of, will bring you to the same ruin as national Israel's loss in the kingdom of God! Add to this Judas Iscariot's evaporated faith, the same for Demas, and those whose candlesticks were removed and their names *'blotted out of The Lamb's Book of Life'*, and you have been shown the multiple saga of evaporated faith both totally and finally!

While it is true that God will not break Covenant with one of His, it does not follow, as they suppose, that we cannot break Covenant with God. To say so is to assume we cannot fall from grace as the Galatians did. Peter said it took perfection of virtues to "never fall", (2Pt 2:10), and our faith, yours and mine, better arrive there. As he said, *'If the righteous are scarcely saved where will the...sinner appear'*? The terms of the Everlasting Covenant made to Abraham and consummated in his seed, (meaning Christ), is to *"walk before Me and be thou perfect"*, Genesis 17:1. Sin is the breaker of our Covenant! God can't sin, so it is true He won't break Covenant. We can sin, but seeing we also can obey the command not to sin, *'let us draw near in full assurance of faith, having our bodies washed with pure water* (baptized), *having our hearts sprinkled from an evil conscience'* (sanctified). Sanctification is the 'sprinkling (cleansing) of an evil conscience', the 'remission of sins', and is the early churches' and the true Christian Baptism! This is the apostles' gospel. Is it yours?

There is little to no fear before the eyes of those who believe Eternal Security! The fear of God has been all but eradicated in today's churches. It is why sin is so prevalent amongst those who claim to have faith! You who claim a covenant must first understand that covenant. God confirmed covenants with men by sacrificing an animal, cutting it in two, the covenanting parties walking between the sacrifice, (Jer 34:18), and swearing to the terms of the covenant, saying, *'May it be unto me as unto this animal if I do not keep the terms of this Covenant'.* Peter knew this when Jesus warned him He would cut him asunder with the unbelievers in Luke 12:46. Do you claim to be in covenant with Almighty God? You must keep the terms of Genesis 17:1 and the command to *'be holy as I AM holy'.* You cannot fear God if you do not believe Him! Peter did!

MacArthur suggests Peter's life was a road map of failure. Shame! It was no such thing. It was a case of one who was slow to believe all things Jesus told him! But believe he did and the baptism John the Baptist foretold was a baptism of the Spirit and fire! Spirit for power and fire for purification! They all went through it and from there warned all who would follow that they *'could not see Jesus unless they were sanctified'* (Heb 12:14). Believing that 'God's warnings do not negate the promises' is the very reason they do not fear God today!

"I will put the fear of Me in their hearts so they will not turn away!" and *"perfect love casts out fear."* The first from Jeremiah and the second from 1John would seem contradictions, but the later refers to having confidence on Judgment Day because a saint has 'perfect love' - meaning they are 'perfectly obeying', maintaining their sanctification. The fear spoken of in Jeremiah is fear of turning away from God. It is not a *placed fear* that makes us saved in sin; on the contrary, it is a fear that obeys *the holy commandment* of the Covenant. The rest of God's council on the Jeremiah passages is: *"and I will write My laws in their inward parts that*

they might not sin against Me." Might is subjunctive and indicates we who are truly in the New Covenant have been provided the means to "stop sinning". That flatly contradicts the notion you can believe 'present tense' sanctification is not for everyday faith, which is everyday obedience to the terms of the covenant.

> *It opposes the radical easy-believeism teaching that genuine Christians can choose to "drop out" of the spiritual growth process and "cease to confess Christianity."*

To "cease to confess Christianity" is to become an apostate. To depart from the truth is turning back in one's heart to Egypt. Remember, the Hebrew writer pointed this out about the Israelites and *God swore in His wrath they would never enter* His rest! This is a warning to us that it could be our fate as well! They broke covenant, (Heb 4:1-2).

> *It is the polar opposite of the brand of theology that makes faith a "historic moment," a one-time "act" that secures heaven, but offers no guarantee the "believer's" earthly life will be changed.*

Half right, as the so-called "sinners prayer" will save no one. Only *"the answer of a good conscience towards God"* can do that. This is explained in 1Peter 3:21-4:1 and Romans 6 and recognized by *'death to sin'*, symbolized *by baptism.* Take note: there is to be no resurrection of the *"old man"* unto sin again and dead men don't sin. Therefore, we are warned *'if we turn back'* He will have no delight in us, (Heb 10:38: Lk 9:62), and it says this of the *"just,"* (a good synonym of a *believer*). As an aside, the thief on the cross was baptized, in his own blood! Baptism is the death of the old man. There is no surer death to sin than having one's sin nature crucified! Remember Hebrews 6:1? The *"doctrines of baptisms"* are plural. The sprinkling of Jesus' blood on our consciences brings life from the death of evil acts. This remission is a present change, not as MacArthur states <u>will be changed</u>. MacArthur believes in the simple idea of 'forgiveness' of sins for now, as confirmed by his claimed "final salvation", which is sin's acts and power eliminated in the *last time.*

    I must note that a Christian can fall by being overcome in a fault and, having done so, can be restored if it is a sin *"not unto death."* (Jam 5:19-20; 1Jn 5:16). However, what is of note in the James passage is that, if they are restored, it is their **soul** that is saved from death. The implication is that a present failure of restoration is that soul's death! It is not speaking of the body suffering death; it says *"a soul"*. There is no security in sin. Mark it well.

> *The Westminster Confession of Faith has defined perseverance as follows:*
>
> *They whom God hath accepted in His Beloved, effectually called and sanctified by his Spirit, can neither totally nor finally fall away from the state of grace; but shall certainly persevere therein to the end, and be eternally saved (chap. 17, sec. 1)*
>
> *This definition does not deny the possibility of miserable failings in one's Christian experience, because the Confession also said,*
>
> *Nevertheless [believers] may, through the temptations of Satan and of the world, the <u>prevalency of corruption remaining</u> in them, and the neglect of the means of their preservation, fall into grievous sins; and for a time continue therein; whereby they incur God's*

> *displeasure, and grieve his Holy Spirit: come to be deprived of some measure of their graces and comforts; have their hearts hardened, and their consciences wounded; hurt and scandalize others, and bring <u>temporal judgments</u> upon themselves (sec. 3).*

This could hardly be called a "holy faith" (Jude 1:20). I note the word <u>temporal</u>. Mr. MacArthur does not address the possibility <u>of dying</u> in that fallen state of <u>temporal judgment</u>, because it would be an obvious admission of an unconditional acceptance by God on Judgment Day. Just as they fault the OSAS 'believers' who use **'a less perfectly framed verbiage'**! (Unless it is an assertion that Perseverance of the Saints means they are unable to die while in a state of sin.) Is this what they mean by their silence? I say it does, otherwise their doctrine, which states *'their need for holiness'*, is contradicted above in this manner: grievous sins, hardened hearts, wounded conscience, scandalizing others. Paul said, concerning the <u>prevalence of corruption remaining</u>, he brings *"his body into subjection lest he become a reprobate/castaway"* (1Cor 9:27). In other words: lost! Just like Jesus warned Peter *he* could be! Their claims and suppositions are all based on a 'saved in your sin gospel'. And that is why they are heretics!

> *Sin is a reality in the believer's experience, so it is clear that insistence on the salvific necessity of a working faith <u>does not include the idea of perfectionism.</u>*

More guile! This is a common practice among the Calvinist, to state a falsehood as fact and then build a doctrine around it. 1John is where we will look at the claim <u>working faith does not include the idea of perfectionism,</u> as 1:8 is the Calvinist's *stronghold* for their false claim that a saint sins "every day in word thought and deed". Perfection, being moral purity, is mandatory for those becoming saints; a definite must for those 'naming Christ' as theirs. First, let me say in the defense of some Calvinists, that not all have claimed the Westminster Catechism's "everyday" doctrine. George Whitfield believed like John Wesley in regard to sin being active in the believer: that it must cease! Other Calvinists as well, like Richard Alderson who taught it in his book NO HOLINESS, NO HEAVEN. However, as with John MacArthur, more believe in a sinning saint than don't.

Now, 1John 1:7-10: *(7)* "But if we walk in the light, as He is in the light, we have fellowship with one another, and the blood of Jesus Christ His Son cleanses us from all sin. *(8)* If we say that we have no sin, we deceive ourselves, and the truth is not in us. *(9)* If we confess our sins, He is faithful and just to forgive* us our sins, and to cleanse us from all unrighteousness."

Light reveals these sins to us, that they must be confessed and repented of, so they can be forgiven and cleansed. Any sin we refuse to forsake, we are walking in. *We cannot say we have no sin* (vs. 8) *and, therefore, are not* required to walk in the light (vs. 7). Many insist verse eight denotes a permanent state of active sin. False teaching of this verse creates the mistaken impression that *'if we say we have no sin'* is actually saying, *'if we say we are not sinning'*.

This would relegate being cleansed from all sin (vs. 7) and the *forgiving** (this is remission, the sending away of sin, rendering its influence and practice void) and cleansing from all unrighteousness (vs. 9) to meaninglessness. It might appear, at first glance, that verse eight in some way annuls the cleansing from all sin. But John distinguishes having sin, or a sin nature, from walking in that nature and committing or doing, sin. This is referred to as walking *'according to flesh'*, as opposed to walking *'according to Spirit'*.

When we repented of the sin that made us conscious of our need of a Savior, leaving these sins at the foot of the cross and turning from darkness to the light, we were 'cleansed' and justified by the blood of Jesus *(for the sins that are past)* in the sight of God. As we walk in the light, sin hidden in our hearts when we first believed, will be exposed by the light. Be very careful how you believe your sins are *'covered by the blood'*. What many mean by this is that any sin they may be committing, or might commit in the future, is automatically *'covered over'*.

By claiming to be *'sinners saved by grace'* some believe they are in compliance with their meaning of 1John 1:8. In other words, although they are still sinning, the wage for their sin has changed; it no longer causes death. Instead of changing us so that we no longer walk in sin - the blood of Jesus has somehow changed the consequences of sin. However, verse seven makes it clear that the blood of Jesus cleanses us if we are in fellowship with Him, walking in the light and not in sin. Verses seven through ten comprise one point in a paragraph, which includes verses five and six. The message does not change: *(vs. 6)* "God is light, with no darkness at all". *We can have fellowship with Him, but not if we walk in darkness (sin)!* (It is, as we are made aware of those hidden sins and turn from them that we are cleansed from all unrighteousness, abiding in the light, having no known sin). This fellowship is accomplished by being forgiven and totally cleansed of confessed and forsaken sin. That is why the conclusion of the paragraph: *(1:10)* "if we say we have not sinned", means in the past.

In his letter, John immediately establishes that the message of the gospel is not abdication to sin. He restates this when he begins chapter two "...These things I write unto you, that you sin not." 1John 1:7 reveals the way to perfection, by being cleansed from all sin, not walking in it. No Christian can walk as Jesus walked, (2:6), while walking in willful sin! Verse nine fixes the state of a believer who deals with his sin properly: he it is who is 'cleansed' from all unrighteousness and in fellowship with the Father and Son and has been known from the beginning as the "sanctified" believer.

This whole Epistle teaches a holy life, known as 'perfect love', which gives us boldness on the day of judgment, because *"as He is so are we **in this world"*** (4:17). This is opposed to the *'at his appearing'* tradition of the Calvinist. The conclusion of the matter is this: we cannot share in the 'divine nature' (union), as promised in 2Peter 1:4, while walking in a false teaching about 1John 1:8. Those of you who want to live in the truth contained in the entire Epistle, your fruit will be righteousness and your Master the same. Let it be so.

OK, what does it mean then "whosoever has the Son has eternal life"? 1John 1:5-7 says in Him is no darkness at all. To walk with Him we can't walk in darkness, and to walk in the light is to forsake all *'sin revealed'*. Verse 8 states we can't say we have no sin and, therefore, have no need to come to the light. It does not say we stay in a perpetual, or even intermittent, state of sin. That would contradict the rest of the epistle. Those who want a license to sin put forth this view as eternal justification, which is a lie from the Pit and yet held by most Evangelicals. The "whole council" of eternal life and being "born again" from this epistle is *'in Christ'* is to be out of sin. Peter called it, obeying the *holy commandment.*

* * *

CHAPTER FIVE

Nevertheless, people steeped in the merely intellectual faith teaching often misunderstand the issue with regard to perseverance. A Christian layman who has embraced easy-believeism teaching wrote me a very graciously worded seventeen-page letter explaining why he rejects the working-faith doctrine. His complaint is that the latter theology "does not seem to allow for anything but highly successful Christian living."

Hodges makes a similar charge:

The belief that every Christian will live a basically successful life until the end is an illusion. It is not supported by the instruction and warnings of the New Testament. It is not surprising that those who do not perceive this aspect of New Testament revelation have impoverished their ability to motivate both themselves and other believers. Tragically, they often fall back on the technique of questioning

> *the salvation of those whose lives seem not to meet Biblical standards. But in the process they undermine the grounds for a believer's assurance and take part 'however unwittingly' in the siege of the Gospel.*
>
> *No advocate of working-faith salvation I am aware of teaches "every Christian will live a basically successful life until the end." Hodges is quite right in saying the NT does not support such a view.*

BELIEVER'S ASSURANCE

The NT does not support such a view? This claim by Hodges and J. MacArthur should remove all doubt that they teach holiness anytime before Christ's appearing! As I said, they deny Luke 1:75 just for a start. Before the Bishop's changed the teaching of *'no sin after baptism'* in 431 A.D., the rudiments of the consequences of falling into sin were so great that it became a common practice to put off baptism until nearly death. Why? Because there was no assurance given in Christendom for a Christian that turned back into any sin, period! You doubt it? You don't know Church History!

Look, this teaching of 'no sin after baptism' was still strongly advocated by some, such as John Chrysostom, well into the fifth century. Jerome didn't like Bishop Chrysostom because Jerome had 'known sin' in his life and Brother Chrysostom did not. The Catholic Church ultimately killed the true gospel by dropping the mandate of "no sin" after baptism, and that is why a century later they found the need to add Purgatory, in order to afford some ASSURANCE. Not to be out done, "The Reformation Fathers" left sin in the camp, but did a one up on the *'seven headed Beast'*; they introduced believer's assurance and took part, 'however unwittingly', in the continuance of a false gospel. (Thus appeared the *'image of the Beast,'* called Protestantism.) *Assurance* in sin is what the one invented and both perpetuate. There is none to be found in the Scriptures or early church history outside of a holy life. Proof in point: a catechumen, (those being discipled in the Faith), were not allowed to partake of the Eucharist or the "love feast" until they were baptized. Why? Baptism, understood as the pivotal point of conversion, was having their sin nature put into remission. This, the apostle Paul testified to in Acts 22:16 concerning his conversion. His believing at the time Jesus blinded him, Ananias affirms by saying, "Be baptized' and **fully wash** [628] **your sins away."** Paul's change of mind (repentance) was towards Jesus! Now, Strong's #628 in this verse is a middle voice imperative, meaning we are commanded to *fully wash our sins* by dying to them with Christ in baptism, water being the symbol and Jesus' blood being the cleansing agent. Having our sins now 'put away' from us by dying to them, they are now 'cleansed', i.e. **we are sanctified!** Because of this we are now justified for, having died to them, they are now <u>past</u> *sins!* Having them in remission we can walk in holiness.

This is plainly not indicating *'baptismal regeneration'* or *'forgiveness of sins by water'*, because the Holy Spirit, which Paul received by the laying on of Ananias' hands, accomplishes that. No, this Christian Baptism is the *putting of sins into remission* by the "power of the Holy Spirit" through a full commitment to it in the waters of baptism, which is *'the answer of a good conscience towards God'* (1Pt 3:21). Thusly, having understood and 'consecrated' to these things, we are truly converted. Converted from death to life, from darkness to light, from sin to righteousness, from righteousness to holiness, from holiness to eternal life. It is eternal life that is received 'in the end' by a continuance in seeking after the same (Rom 2:5-7).

Therefore, continuing to do so, we can have the assurance that *"having died with him we shall also live with Him"*,

2Timothy 2:11. The churches are selling insurance, a 'stay out of hell' pass, which is really just an **Indulgence** by another name. It is why neither the 'merely-intellectual-faith' teachers nor the 'working-faith-salvation' perseverance teachers believe the Words of God that command we be exactly as our Lord and His Father in heaven: *'it is enough that the student be as his Master'*, (Mat 10:25).

    Both commands, *"Be ye perfect as your Father in heaven"* and *"be ye holy for I am holy"*, are put off to the end of their lives. This is not only a *damnable heresy*, but also a denial that the commands are just, which make God's grace impotent and the mandate of the Gospel a future event. Luke 1:75 makes Matthew 1:21's *"from sin"* to be an *"all the days of our lives"* walk, like our Master. God does not practice "affirmative action", however He will affirm us if we *'run according to the rules.'* He works in us to will and to do His good pleasure, *(gives the desire and ability)*, but we must workout our salvation with fear and trembling (Php 2:12). That is how it is brought to completion!

    The Protestant Evangelical and the RCC either allow it now or make sanctification a future event, and in the case of a Calvinist, as MacArthur, proclaim it something Jesus will finish for you in the last days of your life. Mr. MacArthur admits you can't get into God's heaven dirty however, according to him and the other *heretics*, you will stay dirty most, if not all the *days of your life*, more or less, ups and downs. MARK IT WELL, this is license and a saved-in-your-sin 'gospel', which is no gospel at all, but a lie from the Pit. Jude warned of these kinds of latter day false teachers, as did Peter and Paul. They also said, *'men will not always endure sound doctrine, but will heap up teachers to tickle their itching ears'.* This is what has happened to the churches as a whole. Security in any form will sell before God's mandatory commands in the here and now. Look around! The U.S. Government Statistics show gross immorality as common among those who go to church as among those who don't. May I suggest to you, dear reader, that that very thing proves my point.

> *Murray, defending the doctrine of perseverance, acknowledged the difficulties it poses:*
>
> *Experience, observation, biblical history, and certain Scripture passages would appear to provide very strong arguments against the doctrine. Is not the biblical record as well as the history of the church strewn with examples of those who have made shipwreck of the faith?*
>
> *Certainly Scripture is filled with warnings to people in the church lest they should fall away (cf. Heb 6:48; 1Tim 1:18-19; 2Tim 2:16-19). Hodges suggests such warnings prove Christians can fall away: "If anyone supposes that no true Christian could quit, or would quit, they have not been paying attention to the Bible. They need to reread their New Testament, this time, with their eyes open."*

Yes, MacArthur should reread it with his eyes open as well. *"For Demas, in love with this present world, has deserted me and gone to Thessalonica, Crescens has gone to Galatia, Titus to Dalmatia."* (2Tim 4:10)

With eyes open, consider the above verse with Philippians 1:20. Just because some claim Demas was not a true Christian, does not make it so. The evidence is ample that for Calvinism to remain viable, it must annul every evidence there are casualties in a war; we Christians are in a 'spiritual war with principalities and powers and rulers in the heavenly realms'. Do you imagine this war has no victims? The victims of this war are those whose ministers appear as *angels of light,* but inside are *ravenous wolves,* exploiting God's people with lies their vain imaginations have made up, *deceiving and being deceived.* Observe what follows.

> *But God does not contradict Himself. The <u>warning passages do not negate the many promises</u> that believers will persevere:*

Why not assume these inferred promises do not negate the actual warnings? If God <u>does not contradict Himself</u> - and He doesn't—does He then make *idle threats?* Do not the very warnings themselves depict ruin and rejection? Are these warnings without teeth? This is the promotion of Calvinistic license! These implied contradictions then are 'silently' attributed to 'idle threats and become, subliminally, benign! This is *blasphemy and demonic.* Thusly, Perseverance is based on denial and deception.

> *Whoever drinks of the water that I shall give him shall never thirst; but the water that I shall give him shall become in him a well of water springing up to eternal life (John 4:14)*

Assumed to mean you can't go to hell <u>no matter what!</u>

> *I am the bread of life; he who comes to Me shall not hunger, and he who believes in Me shall never thirst (John 6:35)*

Assumed to mean you can never die in willful sin or, if you do, there will be no condemnation.

> *You are not lacking in any gift, awaiting eagerly the revelation of our Lord Jesus Christ, who shall also confirm you <u>in the end,</u>*

1Cor 1:8, *Who also will confirm you until completion, blameless in the day of our Lord Jesus Christ.* (LSJ Greek Lexicon defines what is commonly translated in this verse, *'the end'* #5056, to actually be perfection; full age; completion of the goal; end. There is no definite article there.)

Look, this verse that MacArthur quotes does not read *confirm you in the end*, it reads "*until[2193] completion*. Strong's # 2193 is a preposition and adverb of continuance and does not imply confirmation in or at the end, rather "continuing from now to an end". The Lord will confirm in the end those who *"died with Him to sin"*, (Rom 6:2-3), and *"rose like Him"* to be in sin no more in this life. Jesus' teaches to be His disciples *'we must be free of sin,'* then we can *remain in the house forever* (Jn 8:35). This is the true perseverance of the saints, persevering (continuing) in holiness. But this is not what they teach perseverance to be. They are wolves in sheep's clothing, distorters of truth *'from which they have wandered.'*

In earlier days we can find the Calvinist stating that a saint had to be without sin at least before they died, even if it was only a day or an hour before. This can be discovered in books like George MacDonald's, and in other writings. Seeing they understood that *without holiness no man will see the Lord*, and believing it had to happen before they died, John Wesley used to ask them, "Why not a week before they die? Or a year, or ten years?" It only goes to show that the desire to keep their sin to the last is the real problem and motive. As Ezekiel 14:4 points out, as does 2Thessolonians 2:10-11, the peril of this desire.

> . . . *blameless in the day* of our Lord Jesus Christ. God is faithful,* through whom you were called into fellowship with His Son, Jesus Christ our Lord (1Cor 1:7-9).

> *May the God of peace Himself <u>sanctify you entirely</u>: and may your spirit and soul and body be <u>preserved</u> complete, without blame at the <u>coming of our</u> Lord Jesus Christ. <u>Faithful is He who calls you, and He also will bring it to pass</u> (1Thess 5:23-24).*

Preservation *in* His coming is taken to mean *'limited to* His appearing', which could just as easily not include beyond (1Cor 1:8; 1Thes 5:23). Blamelessness, being without spot or wrinkle or any such thing, does seem to be promoted here at last. But alas, John MacArthur and others choose the verses that suggest it only really happens when the Lord appears. It corrupts the imperative to be holy now, for there is no verse that reads 'become holy at His appearing'. So the lie goes on. It is a *'bruise to His heel'*. MacArthur's *blameless <u>in the day</u> does not necessarily mean <u>before</u> the day!

* * *

CHAPTER SIX

> *They went out from us, but they were not really of us; for if they had been of us, they would have remained with us; but they went out, in order that it might be shown that they all are not of us (1John 2:19).*

The Catholic Church also quotes this about the Protestant churches, suggesting that if you don't agree to their twisting of the Word, you don't belong 'to Christ.

> *Now unto him that is able to keep you from falling, and to present you faultless before the presence of his glory with exceeding joy, to the only wise God our Saviour, be glory and majesty, dominion and power, both now and forever. Amen (Jude 24-25, KJV, emphasis added in all citations).*

Horne observed,

THE CHURCHES' FOLLY

> *It is noteworthy that when Jude exhorts us to keep ourselves in the love of God (v. 21) he concludes <u>with a doxology</u> for Him who is able to <u>keep us from falling</u> and who will present us without blemish before the presence of His glory (v. 24). The warning passages are means, which God uses in our life to <u>accomplish His purpose in grace</u>.*

Such psychobabble! His purpose in grace is according to the Covenant of Grace, which is Christ *in* us manifesting His life *through* us. And that life was not one that didn't include *biblical/divine/moral* perfection. Deceivers love to make claims that will make their followers capable of being *'twice the sons of hell as they are'*. MacArthur quotes 'Jesus is <u>able to keep you from falling</u>', why then does a Calvinist insist on <u>the rudiments of corruption</u> prevailing over the remission of sins? Is this more double speaking? If He's able by His grace, (or any other means for that matter), why are they constantly falling into sin? It is one thing to quote a scripture and quite another to believe it. **"Prevailing corruption"** is what J. MacArthur and his diabolical Westminster Catechism promotes! Let me say it again, **Sin prevailing over grace** is what they are selling! To buy this is to purchase death! Remember the word the Lord gave:

"*Some love what they think My Word says, but they do not love the Truth. For when My Word speaks contrary to the doctrines and traditions of men they refuse My Word, which they profess to love.*"

A doxology is a liturgical formula for praise to God. Indeed, Biblical passages are to get us "*to come to our senses and stop sinning*" (1Cor 15:34). It is ludicrous to claim Jude's doxology after all those pronouncements of sin continuing to be actively present in some measure everyday in word, thought *and* deed in a saint's life! This leaves praise only at the Lord's appearing. Is there anybody to praise Him now *'for keeping that which has been committed unto Him against that Day'*? Just because they have admitted He is able to present us blameless/faultless "at" His appearing, does not praise the Lord's ability to keep us in the present!

As a matter of fact, I find it an insult to the Spirit of Grace! Does not Paul state *'all the righteous requirements of the law are,* (therefore can be), *fully met in us who walk according to Spirit'*? Indeed he does, so why all this hedging on the issue? It is a silent denial of Jesus' ability. Does not that really explain it in light of Luke 1:75? The *"idol of iniquity"* in front of the eyes of those who even remotely suggest Jesus is not able to keep you from falling NOW is exposed. Their argument will now be loudly proclaimed, "Well, *Paul* never got over his weakness to sin." You see, even though he said he did in *Romans 8:2,* they won't believe him. If you did, you would not give the Lord rest day or night until you received the *promise of sharing in the Divine Nature!* You know, that nature that Mr. MacArthur has suggested, (in so many words right from the beginning), Peter never had in this world.

> *And, it could be added, the warning passages like Jude 21 reveal that the writers of Scripture were very keen to alert those whose hope of salvation might be grounded in a spurious faith. Obviously the apostolic authors were not laboring under the illusion that every person in the churches to whom they were writing was genuinely converted.*

And you are suggesting even those who are will only become blameless at His appearing. And let us not forget that Jude was writing to the saints, *(those that are sanctified),* which you cannot be if grounded in a "spurious faith". The whole statement above is smoke and mirrors in an attempt to denigrate God's warnings!

ONCE SAVED, ALWAYS SAVED?

It is crucial to understand what the biblical doctrine of perseverance does not mean. It does not mean that people who "accept Christ" can then live any way they please without fear of hell. The expression "eternal security" is often used in this sense, as is "once saved, always saved" Kendall, arguing for the latter phrase, defines its meaning thus:

"Whoever once truly believes that Jesus was raised from the dead, and confesses that Jesus is Lord, will go to heaven when he dies. But I will not stop there. Such a person will go to heaven when he dies no matter what work (or lack of work) may accompany such faith.

This kind of gospel, though MacArthur is not concurring to this degree, is what is most widely held by today's big name teachers from radio and TV fame, along with a very large host of individual churches, that have all said *'when Jesus comes he will take you with him, even if you're walking in known sin'.* Yes, most of America's churches are bankrupt, as the Government itself, and for the same reason, *lawlessness.* While the Government breaks its own laws, the churches violate Christ's Law. Lawlessness and deception, the two main signs given for the *last of days*, is mainstream.

Kendall also writes, "I hope no one will take this as an attack on the Westminster Confession. It is not that" But is precisely that! Kendall expressly argues against Westminster's assertion that faith cannot fail. He believes faith is best characterized as a

> *single look: "one need only see the Sin Bearer once to be saved." This is a full-scale assault against the doctrine of perseverance affirmed in the Westminster Confession. Worse, it subverts Scripture itself. Unfortunately, it is a view that has come to be widely believed by Christians today.*

While Calvinists like Mr. MacArthur disagree in particular, he and others still hold to a sinning-saint mentality until the Appearing. Their Catechism is the defining truth of the ages to them, which they use to twist the Scriptures. A case in point is Murray being quoted below on 'The Security of the Believer', which neither he nor MacArthur acknowledge as wrong, only that it is not as *exact* as their 'perseverance of the saints'. The fact remains the same, even though only by degree, that they both provide license; either a sinning saint goes in anyway and only loses some reward, or the sinning saint has his sin practice removed near death and loses nothing.

> *– Not because the latter is wrong in itself, but because the other formula is much more carefully and inclusively framed.–*

"More carefully framed" to keep the deception going that you can be a 'sinning saint', even though there is no such thing in the Word, in Webster's Dictionary, in Strong's Lexicon or early Church teaching. Never mind the facts, they would just have you believe their Westminster Catechism is right and all else wrong. Behold:

> *Murray, noting this trend nearly forty years ago, defended the expression "perseverance of the saints":*

> *It is not in the best interests of the doctrine involved to substitute the designation, "The Security of the Believer," not because the latter is wrong in itself but because the other formula is much more carefully and inclusively framed . . . It is not true that the believer is secure however much he may fall into sin and unfaithfulness. Why is this not true? It is not true because it sets up an impossible combination. It is true that a believer sins; he may fall into grievous sin and backslide for lengthy periods. But it is also true that a believer cannot abandon himself to sin; he cannot come under the dominion of sin; he cannot be guilty of certain kinds of unfaithfulness.*

Lengthy periods of certain kinds of unfaithfulness is not considered coming under the dominion of sin? All right! Is this 'common knowledge' yet? So why not go on an extended *gross immorality* binge? Let's say, well, how about for a lengthy period? Then all we have to do is go to *Confession* or attend a Sunday service to have *Absolution* pronounced over us. You say, "That falls under certain kinds of unfaithfulness". Really? How do you define certain kinds? How do you define lengthy periods? What sin committed did not dominate good behavior? This psychobabble is what is considered "a formula much more carefully and inclusively framed"? May God help us!

> *The truth is that the faith of Jesus Christ is always respective of the life of holiness and fidelity. And so it is never proper to think of a believer irrespective of the fruits in faith and holiness.*

Did you digest that claim? Did you understand the truth of "always *respective* of holiness" being handed out with the left hand and being pulled back with the right? The fruits of faith and holiness, it is true, is what we should expect a believer to manifest! But Jesus said, *"a bad tree does not produce good fruit nor does a good tree produce bad fruit."* *"It is by their fruit you will know them!"* Therefore, Murray and MacArthur are wrong to teach Christians will and can have lengthy periods or seasons of sin. This is the acceptance of a professing believer irrespective of the fruits in faith and holiness! So to say it is never proper to think of a Christian without the fruits in faith and holiness and then do that very thing, is double-speak! (The true literal translation of their above statement is this: you are positionally sanctified in your everyday sin irrespective of the fruits of faith and holiness.) Thus the popularity of Perseverance of the Saints, which is truly the fruit of darkness!

> *To say that a believer is secure whatever may be the extent of his addiction to sin in his subsequent life is to abstract faith in Christ from its very definition and it ministers to that abuse which turns the grace of God into lasciviousness. The doctrine of perseverance is the doctrine that believers persevere . . . It is not at all that they will be saved irrespective of the their perseverance or their continuance, but that they will assuredly persevere. Consequently the security that is theirs is inseparable from their perseverance. Is this not what Jesus said? "He than endureth to the end, the same shall be saved." Let us not then take refuge in our sloth or encouragement in our lust from the abused doctrine of the security of the believer. But let us appreciate the*

> *doctrine of the perseverance of the saints and recognize that we may entertain the faith of our security in Christ only as we persevere in faith and holiness to the end.*

Murray has already said a saint can be in sin for lengthy periods and MacArthur, teaching the same security and assurance in sin, now throws in: But let us appreciate the doctrine of the perseverance of the saints and recognize that we may entertain the faith of our security in Christ only as we persevere in faith and holiness to the end. All through this discourse we have been reading Calvinism by MacArthur asserting *at the end.* So to hide the truth that their Catechism teaches no experiential holiness, they throw in a quote by Murray that is to distract you from what they really teach, i.e. a saint sinning every day of his life until Jesus appears. This is the truth about Calvinism and all the rest is just babble.

> *Any doctrine of eternal security that leaves out perseverance distorts the doctrine of salvation itself. Heaven without holiness ignores the whole purpose for which God chose and redeemed His people:*

Again they are saying holiness is really only for Heaven, but very smoothly being said! (Note the underlined statement below.) What does it say? Like Him when He appears is what they teach; not like Him now. Do you see their subterfuge? Just because they add, *"he who has this hope purifies himself just as Christ is pure,"* doesn't change the fact that they already negated it by saying "like Him when He appears." Doublespeak indeed, deceptive to the unlearned and the reason I labor to expose their deception.

> *God elected us for this very purpose. "He chose us in him [Christ] before the creation*

of the world to be holy and blameless in his sight" (Eph. 1:4). We were predestinated to be conformed to the image of Christ in all His spotless purity (Rom. 8:29). This divine choice makes it certain that we shall be like Him when He appears (1John 3:2). From this fact, John deduces that everyone who has this hope in him purifies himself just as Christ is pure (1John 3:3). His use of the word "everyone" makes it quite certain that those who do not purify themselves will not see Christ, nor be like Him. By their lack of holiness they prove that they were not so predestinated. The apostle thus deals a crushing blow to Antinomianism.

This claim to be holy to see the Lord was with some Calvinists in the past, but now they hand it out with the left hand while taking it back with the right. Mr. MacArthur hedges on Jesus being able to keep us from *'all wrong'*, at least in the respect that Luke 1:75 proclaims the Covenant. (Theirs is the teaching of the 'unsuccessful' Christian.) Again, they must assume the saint can't die until Jesus appears. Where do any of them teach the Covenant is *'to be in holiness all the days of our life'*? They hint at it, but will not support the Holy Spirit's "he that is born of God does not sin." Nowhere in Reformed Theology! (Close does not count, but it does deceive.)

Predestinated to be conformed is never meant by them to be "today". Neither it nor they ever state it to be mandatory *"while it is called today"*! Ahora mismo! Right now, not later. If it can be later then it can be anytime, all the way up to His return.

This brings us back to the practice that began so many centuries ago – putting off one's baptism till near death – leaving the believer in sin till then. The Protestant calls it a 'sinning saint.' A Catholic knows this is an oxymoron yet still offers some assurance for their 'faithful' - (regular attendees and givers of the tithe) - called Purgatory. The early church did not hold this belief, because the opposite was taught! The Didaché, being the earliest known church Catechism, said this: *"the whole time of your sojourn here will be for naught unless you are found perfect in the end."* I have already listed the scriptures that make *moral perfection,* (the Bible's *perfect),* mandatory. Does the Didaché agree? Or does it agree with the teaching of Purgatory? Does *"it is appointed unto man once to die and after this the judgment"* agree with the Didaché (Heb 9:27)? Nineteenth century Bishop Lightfoot of the Church of England believed the Didaché to be canonical; so do I, because it is totally compatible with the Word.

While it is reported in the Word that babes in Christ might sin, it does not suggest that we remain babes for 20 or 40 years and only grow into *"young men"* or *"old men"* in the faith when Jesus appears, as MacArthur suggests. If he wasn't suggesting this, wouldn't he plainly state the 'soul must be lost in order for it to be saved'. This is death to the fallen nature, in order for us to live above sin. I cannot find Mr. MacArthur going there. He comes close at times, but close counts in horseshoes not in 'everyday of our life' holiness. The apostle John says they have overcome the evil one, i.e. they have *stopped* sinning (1Jn 3:8). This verse is as valid as 1:8, is it not? At what point in our life are we saved from sin? Death? His appearing? Or according to the command: now and till the end?

※ ※ ※

CHAPTER SEVEN

God's own holiness thus requires perseverance. "God's grace insures our persevering but this does not make it any less our persevering." Believers cannot acquire "the prize of the upward call of God in Christ Jesus" unless they "press on toward the goal" (Phil 3:14). But as they "work out [their] salvation with fear and trembling" (Phil 2:12), they find that "it is God who is at work in [them], both to will and work for His good pleasure" (Phil 2:13).

"THE OUTCOME OF YOUR FAITH"

Perhaps no apostle understood better than Peter the keeping power of God in the life of an inconsistent believer. God had preserved him and matured him through every kind of faux pas and failure, including severe sin and compromise even repeated denials of the Lord accompanied by cursing and swearing! (Matt 26:69-75)

THE CHURCHES' FOLLY

The subtlety of the Serpent does not slumber. Here at the midsection of his Journal, Mr. MacArthur brings Peter back into the fore. Why? As before, the implication is Peter remained an inconsistent believer. Why? He reiterates Peter's two early known failings in order to perpetuate the promotion of a lifetime of preserving in failure. This author has been careful to point out that with God there is mercy. God makes provision for repentance and offers remittance of sin. However there is a time, called *Today*, that God requires purification of our lives. This very thing the churches have polluted, in spite of their **feigned** insistence of a holy life and the fruits of faith! In their holding Perseverance up they bring down obedience to the gospel. How far do you think the apostles' teaching of mandatory holiness would have gotten if they themselves were in active sin?

I wonder how long it will take them to find out that God Almighty considered even Old Testament saints, like Job, Noah and Daniel, **holy** before Pentecost and even before His first appearing. (Ezk 14:14, 20)

Oh! How God's forbearance and mercy really are displayed to all creation in this matter. Know this and mark it well: Matthew 7:23 and Luke 13:23-28 were spoken to those calling Him Lord. Yet, they could not go in because they did lawlessness, which is sin. Does that mean we cannot repent of all known sin now and avoid that final rejection? Or is it suggesting that conversion allows for ongoing sin? Absolutely not! We must turn from *all* unrighteousness while "it is called today". This is the Law and the Testimony, yes, and the Gospel.

> *Yet the power of God kept Peter in faith despite his own failures. It is therefore appropriate that he become the instrument of the Holy Spirit used to pen the following glorious promise:*

Blessed be the God and Father of our Lord Jesus Christ, who according to His great mercy has caused us to be born again to a living hope through the resurrection of Jesus Christ from the dead, to obtain an inheritance which is imperishable and undefiled and will not fade away, reserved in heaven for you, who are protected by the power of God through faith for a salvation ready to be revealed in the last time. In this you greatly rejoice, even though now for a little while, if necessary, you have been distressed by various trials, that the proof of your faith, being more precious than gold which is perishable, even though tested by fire, may be found to result in praise and glory and honor at the revelation of Jesus Christ; and though you have not seen Him, you love Him, and though you do not see Him now, but believe in Him, you greatly rejoice with joy inexpressible and full of glory, obtaining as the outcome of your faith the salvation of your souls (1Pet 1:3-9)

Peter was writing to scattered believers living in Asia Minor. They were facing a horrible persecution that had begun at Rome and was spreading through the Roman Empire. After the city of Rome burned, Nero had blamed Christians for the disaster. Gradually believers everywhere were becoming targets of tremendous persecution. These people feared for their lives, and they feared they would fail if put to the test for their faith.

Peter wrote this epistle to encourage them. He reminded them that they were aliens in this

> *world, citizens of heaven, a royal aristocracy, children of God, residents of an unearthly kingdom, living stones, a holy priesthood, and a people for God's own possession. Peter told them they were not to fear the threats, they were not to be intimidated, they were not to be troubled by the world's animosity, and they were not to be afraid when they suffered.*
>
> *Why? Because Christians are "protected by the power of God through faith." Instead of giving them doses of sympathy and commiseration, Peter pointed them to their <u>absolute security as believers</u>:*

Here is a mixture of truth and error. Persecution was often the norm in the early church and one of the results Church historians referred to was the Lapsi. The Lapsi were those who, after conversion and baptism, when confronted with a painful death *'lost their faith'* that God would sustain them through the trial and *'denied the Faith'* because of fear! The Church initially considered this loss of faith as final. The Overseers endeavored for a time to hold the line on Jesus' requirement of *'remaining faithful unto death to inherit eternal life'*. But pressure from those who did remain faithful finally prevailed over Church leaders, and the Lapsi were allowed back in the Church! *"There is a sin unto death"* and 'loss of faith' was considered one of those sins! To teach that this 'sin of unfaithfulness' does not negate the Calvinist's "absolute security" is an example of men's doctrines over the Lord's commandment! There is no 'absolute security' in sin. MacArthur's claim of this kind of security is not what the Word of God says. It says *'**IF** you remain faithful to the end, not denying Him before men, you will be saved'*, and that does not spell 'absolute'. The section above – which is actually on *persecution* -- is implying that in 'denying Jesus' you still maintain absolute security. This is a grievous sore! Peter's night of denials were not "unto death" because he repented of his denial and never denied His Lord again, remaining faithful through grievous trials – (not through grievous sin). Peter's restoration was part of his conversion, which heretofore, had not transpired. Why point out the man of failure when right along side there is an example of steadfastness and uprightness: John.

The above by MacArthur does reveal what Christ has done and also implies what he will do even if, as Peter, we deny Him. However, this denying is not faith and love! Faithfulness unto death was what the Lord taught. Judas' sorrow in his denial was a worldly sorrow and it led to death. Peters' denial was accompanied with a godly sorrow, which *"leads to repentance and needs not to be repented of"* again! This will result in *"the outcome of your faith being the salvation of your souls."* (I address Biblical conditions for sin in the 'babes' † in Christ further on). Peter's denial was before his conversion, but the Lapsi were those who had already been converted. This conversion is to be recognized now, (as it was then), *"by their fruit"*, which results from our dying to self so we can become *'Christ's seed'* (Gal 3:14, 16, 29). This requires the indwelling of the Holy Spirit, which is how 'spiritual fruit' grows. The promised Spirit of Holiness has been available to the Christian since Pentecost. Therefore, the Lapsi's denial and Peter's denial are apples and oranges.

※ ※ ※

CHAPTER EIGHT

He knew they might be losing all their earthly possessions and even their lives, but he wanted them to know they would never lose what they had in Christ. (1) Their heavenly inheritance was guaranteed. (2) They were being kept by divine power. (3) Their faith would endure through anything. (4) They would persevere through their trials and be found worthy at the end. (5) Their love for Christ would remain intact. (6) Even now, in the midst of their difficulties, God would provide the spiritual deliverance they needed, according to His eternal plan. An explanation of those six means of perseverance will sum up how God sustains every Christian.

Many professed Christ and even lived holy lives - (remember, the Church taught no sin after baptism) - but some of those very righteous Christians often could not remain faithful unto death. If we can only know who a Christian is after they die, what does that do to Jesus words, *"By their fruit you will know them"?* Is it a spiritual fruit to die in the body? Of course not. So Jesus meant while we live. The faithfulness unto death is not the evidence of a Christian; rather it is the outcome of their fruit. *"Though I offer my body to be burned, yet have not love, it profits me nothing."* A guaranteed inheritance is kept for those who are faithful unto death!

> *Christians are born again to a living hope. "God . .0020. has caused us to be born again to a living hope through the resurrection of Jesus Christ from the dead to obtain an inheritance which is imperishable and undefiled and will not fade away, reserved in heaven for you" (vv.3-4). Every Christian is born again to a living hope 'that is, a hope that is perpetually alive, a hope that cannot die. Peter seems to be making a contrast to mere human hope, which is always a dying or a dead hope. Human hopes and dreams inevitably fade and ultimately disappoint. That is why Paul told the Corinthians, "If we have hoped in Christ in this life only, we are of all men most to be pitied" (1Cor 15:19). This living hope in Christ cannot die. God guarantees that it will finally* come to a complete and total, glorious eternal fulfillment. "This hope we have as an anchor of the soul, a hope both sure and steadfast" (Heb 6:19).*
>
> *That has clear implications beyond the normal concept of eternal security. Again, the point is not only that Christians are saved forever and safe from hell, no matter what. It means more than that: Christian hope does not die.*

This finally,* claimed to always become total, has been answered. Here is the deception plainly revealed again. Calvinists really do believe the sinning saint is *saved from HELL* and not from sin! What this proves is that no matter how much verbiage is strung across the page and how many verbal gymnastics are used in their denial, given enough time and space a Calvinist will hang himself with his own words, as has been done here many times! The Westminster Catechism states that justification removes the guilt and condemnation of sin, but it does not state justification is *"for the sins that **are past**"*. For sins to be *past sins* they must remain in the past! Calvinism teaches justification to include present and future sins, leaving sin alive in a believer. The above shows, from their 'commandments of men' and the 'tradition of their elders', they do not believe justification or sanctification really sets the **'slave free from sin'** until near death or at Jesus' appearing.

Yes, as Mr. MacArthur says, it means more than this. Saved forever and safe from hell *no matter what* really means Jesus was a liar. Oh yes, it does! This promotion, of 'keeping your idol of iniquity in front of your face' and, like the Pharisees, replacing God's WORD with a false Catechism, must stop. Yes, I meant you put it before Jesus by teaching contrary to Him who said, *"Go and sin no more!"* This was not a suggestion, nor does He defer to the Calvinist's Westminster Catechism.

> *Christian faith will not fail. That is the heart of the doctrine of perseverance.*

Translation: the heart of perseverance is SIN CAN STAY, but we will teach it sinning *saints*. This is the **embodiment of Perseverance of the Saints!** Calvinists are *'ever learning but never able to come to the knowledge'* of the truth that saves out of sin every day. That is really what is happening in the Calvinist's covenant, which is opposed to Luke 1:68-75, the real Covenant God made for all time!

> *But this passage **does** teach eternal security as well.*

Eternal Security no matter what means "no matter what". So, let's keep doing verbal gymnastics until a thing often repeated becomes common knowledge. (Meaning, a lie becomes the truth to the deceived.)

> *Christians are guaranteed an inheritance,*

Yes, we know: no matter what. Never mind calling it license, we'll deny it with more contradictory words in a more perfectly framed verbiage that will deceive the unlearned. It makes for such a web that those who attempt to expose it will either bore the hearer to death or put them to sleep.

> *which is imperishable and undefiled and will not fade away, reserved in heaven" (v.4).*

BABES IN CHRIST

Yes, it's reserved in heaven for those who obey the Lord and stop sinning all the days of their life in order to receive the imperishable inheritance, (Rom 2:6-8, 6:8; Heb 5:9). 'If *we sin we have an advocate with the Father, Jesus Christ the righteous,*' (1Jn 2:1b). When taken in context with verses 7-8, it shows that *'babes in Christ'* ✝ have not yet *'overcome the evil one'*. Further on John teaches *'young men'* and the *'fathers'* have. As Paul taught in 1Corinthians 15:34, they **HAVE** *'come to their senses and stopped sinning!'* John describes this sensibleness as *'keeping oneself'* (1Jn 5:18). This the Church believed from the apostles until the Overseers officially departed the truth in 431 A.D. It has survived to this very day by being covered over with Purgatory, Perseverance and Eternal Security, full of priestcraft and trickery. Providing a false hope is providing no hope at all.

> *Unlike everything in this life, which may be corrupted, decay, grow old, rust, corrode, be stolen, or lose its value, an inheritance is reserved for Christians incorruptible, undefiled, and unfading. A full inheritance will one day be the culmination of the living hope of Christians. It is "reserved in heaven" "not like a hotel reservation which may be unexpectedly cancelled, but permanently and unchangeably."*

The obedient believer, who is the true Christian, has an *inheritance* in heaven, where it remains. It is reserved in heaven: But on what grounds? The word in this verse translated 'reserved' in the KJV means "to keep an eye on..." Yes, a true Christian can look forward to an inheritance. Who it is kept for is defined as the sentence finishes in the next verse, *for you* "...those kept in God's power, through faith...' This word 'kept' is *guarded/being held in subjection*. It is through our faith in Him that we are kept in subjection to His power. Mr. MacArthur has selected the outcome of Peter's life as the example that faith can never totally fail, then makes that the guarantee that no faith can fail. He continues building on that belief to guarantee heaven to all who ever had 'faith'.

Demas' faith failed, and a whole host of others who have turned back and walked with the Lord, faithful no more. The determining element is **subjection** *"through faith". "...To present you holy and unblameable and unreproveable in his sight,* **If** *ye continue in the faith..."* (Col 1:22-23) *"...Know, that no whoremonger, nor unclean person, nor covetous man, who is an idolater, has any inheritance in the kingdom of Christ and of God."* (Eph 5:5) An inheritance guaranteed to be undefiled, imperishable and that will not vanish away because it is a heavenly inheritance. Unfortunately, it is not, (as Mr. MacArthur would have us believe), like a reservation that can never be canceled.

To believe unto salvation is to have the subjection saving faith manifests. Not as these teachers suppose it to mean: Christ's faith will save you in your sin. You are kept by *your work of faith.* It is totally bogus to claim an irrevocable reservation. This is also why they deny free will. (*Oh, how deceived are men willing to be for their idol of Security in Sin!*) Subsequent to the "reserved in heaven" verse is verse 2 of 1Peter 1, *"Elect according to the foreknowledge of God the Father, in sanctification of spirit to obedience and sprinkling of the blood of Jesus Christ: Grace unto you, and peace, be multiplied."* MacArthur has failed to point out that *foreknowledge* of the Elect is God already knowing who will or will not become *sanctified to obedience.* Their <u>guaranteed inheritance</u> is based on predestination without a present sanctified obedience! (Suggesting there is a heavenly lotto, which leaves foreknowledge out of the predestination equation.)

We are able to determine this from the context, which refers back to our 'obedience' spoken of in this manner, 1Peter 1:22: *"Seeing ye have purified your souls in obedience of the truth through spirit..."* Subjection is that obedience. 1Peter 1:15-17: *"so be ye holy in all manner of **behavior**; because it is written, be ye holy; for I am holy. And if ye call on the Father, who without respect of persons judgeth according to every man's work, pass the time of your sojourning here in fear:"* Does this not confirm Hebrews 5:9 that says Jesus is the savior only of those who obey Him? And Peter proclaims it to be primarily obeying *'the holy commandment'.* How can we know that 'holy commandment' is *"sin no more?"* By the very context of this chapter, *"Be ye holy!"* (1Pt 1:16) This imperative should be the end to their objection. Peter, the Lord and God have spoken. The false teachers are exposed!

Contrary to MacArthur's claim, a guarantee that disobedient children can inherit does not exist.

> *Christians still alive have already received part of that inheritance. Ephesians 1:13-14 says, "[Having] believed, you were sealed in Him with the Holy Spirit of promise,*

On what basis are we sealed? Believing, you say? I ask where is believing defined? Compare Romans 12:1's *"reasonable worship"* with the following in 2Timothy 2:19, *"But the foundation that God has laid is solid. On it is this seal, "The Lord knows who his people are. So everyone who worships the Lord **must** turn away from iniquity."* I ask then, where is no matter what to be found in that verse? Many I have talked to say they are turning away every day and they add, 'I sin *everyday*, so I confess sin everyday.' Might have Jesus been telling the truth when he said not everyone who says 'Lord, Lord' will enter? But only those *"who do the will of my Father in heaven"*. What is the mandatory will that must be done in order to have His Seal on us? "Do not knowingly violate a command." Until when? His appearing or all the days of your life? The wrong choice can be fatal. The Churches cannot save us, only Jesus can.

> *who is given as a pledge of our inheritance, with a view to the redemption of God's own possession, to the praise of His glory" (cf. 2Cor 1:22:5:5). "Pledge" in v.14 comes from the Greek word arrhabon, which means "down payment." When a person first believes, the Holy Spirit Himself moves into that person's heart. He is the security deposit on eternal salvation for Christians. He is an advance on the Christian's inheritance. He is the guarantee that God will finish the work He has*

> *started. "And do not grieve the Holy Spirit of God by whom you were sealed for the day of redemption" (Eph 4:30, emphasis added.*

THE GIVEN SEAL

It seems good to note here that a struggling believer, one called a *'bruised reed and a smoldering wick'*, has a kind and gracious God. However, what 'eternal security' advocates deny is God does not overlook sin indefinitely. I quantify it thusly: *"He who being often reproved and hardeneth his heart shall suddenly be cutoff and that without remedy."* I inserted this explanation here to clarify that God's seal is not guaranteed permanent or irrevocable as is claimed. The word 'earnest' is a legal term for a part of the purchase price given in pledge, a down payment or deposit. In a real estate transaction, for instance, the prospective buyer's earnest money is deposited with the agent until the deal is closed in escrow and the money and property exchanged. If the seller changes his mind, deciding not to sell, the deposit *reverts to the buyer.*

If we use this illustration for the earnest of our inheritance, we could look at it this way: God is the buyer, we are the seller. The Holy Spirit, the seed of Christ, remains as a deposit until God takes physical possession, or raises us up at the last day. He gives us this deposit when we make our promise to 'sell out' to Him, which calls for us to commit our will to His, (baptism representing our acceptance of the terms). We are then entered into covenant, the promises being exchanged. Eternal life is the final payment promised to those who abide in Him, remain under the terms of the covenant.

Because it is the Holy Spirit given as the earnest, some believe the covenant can never be broken. We can be assured that God is faithful and will never be the one who breaks it; He is not willing that any should perish. However, if we become weary in well doing and take back to ourselves the life we had promised to God, we break covenant.

Mr. MacArthur assumes at this point that there is a certainty of an inheritance, even if you break covenant. This is assumed on their false definition of the word "saved"; they believe they are 'saved from hell, no matter what'! Teaching it to mean from 'guilt and condemnation', i.e. from hell, they imagine you can't get saved but once or you weren't saved in the first place! (John MacArthur becomes in this respect what he calls an intellectual faith-teacher.) As shown earlier in this book, 'saved' is away from sin, not 'saved in sin from hell'. These misunderstandings happen when people have erroneous concepts of words.

✳ ✳ ✳

CHAPTER NINE

Christians are kept by God's own power. "[We are] protected by the power of God through faith for a salvation ready to be revealed in the last time" (v.5). That is a rich statement, guaranteeing the consummation of every believer's eternal salvation. The phrase, "a salvation ready to be revealed in the last time," speaks of <u>full and final salvation</u> the curse of the law, the <u>power and presence</u> of sin, all decay, every stain of iniquity, all temptation, all grief, all pain, all death, all punishment, all judgment, and all wrath. God has begun this work in Christians already, and He will thoroughly complete it (cf. Phil 1:6)

The above rendering of salvation is the promotion of a 'powerless gospel'. Whereas, <u>final salvation</u> is our glorification given at His appearing. According to Matthew 1:21 and Luke 1:75, it is deliverance from the *power* and, (Rom 6:14), the *dominion of sin*, which is 'full' salvation here. That is what 'being saved' means! The Calvinists believe they possess eternal life now while walking in known sin. Whereas we can know we have eternal life when we are *in* Christ (Rom 8:2), we do not receive it ourselves until part two, which is eternal life received 'in the end'. [Mat 10:22, 13:49, 24:13, Rom 6:21, 22, 14:9; 2Cor 2:9; 1Pt 1:9, 4:17; Rev 2:26, (this final verse strongly indicates a present continual holiness that Luke 1:75 makes definitive)].

MacArthur misleads by saying full and final salvation is only revealed in the last time, the power and presence of sin broken then. The work God thoroughly completes, (cf. Php 1:6), is the glorification that comes with eternal life! Therefore, the Gospel does not support a lifetime of work to deliver us from sin that we walk in 'more or less' till our death or Christ's appearing. Salvation is passing from the kingdom of Satan to the kingdom of Christ, which is the 'present deliverance' from the acts of sin (Acts 26:18; Jn 5:25). This is what Jesus gives to those who obey Him. Again, theirs is **THE CHURCHES' FOLLY.**

> *Earlier in the sentence is this phrase: "you . . . are protected by the power of God through faith". Christians are protected by the power of a supreme, omnipotent, sovereign, omniscient, almighty God. The verb tense speaks of continuous action. Even now believers are being protected.*
>
> *"Neither death, nor life, nor angels, nor principalities, nor things present, nor things to come, nor powers, nor height, nor depth, nor any other created thing, shall be able to separate us from the love of God, which is in Christ Jesus our Lord" (Rom 8:38-39). "If God be for us, who can be against us?" (Rom 8:31, KJV)*

This issue of being separated from the love of God is addressed in chapter ten.

> *"[He] is able to keep you from stumbling,*

1Corinthians 10:13 declares the same and states we must therefore chose not to sin. He makes the way of escape; we must take it. That is a 'working faith'.

> *and to make you stand in the presence of His glory blameless with great joy" (Jude 24).*

That is how He makes us stand NOW to the uttermost, but not without great difficulty and through faith that obeys (Heb 3:19; Lk 13:20; Acts 14:22).

> *Furthermore, Christians are protected through faith. Continued faith in Christ is the instrument of God's sustaining work. God did not save Christians apart from faith, and He does not keep them apart from faith. Our faith is God's gift, and through His protecting power He preserves it and nurtures it. The maintenance of a Christian's faith is as much His work as every other aspect of salvation. <u>Faith is kindled and driven and maintained and fortified by God's grace.</u>*

Actually, this is askew. It is not grace that fortifies faith, but faith that enables God's grace to operate in and through us! It is by grace, (not mercy), we are saved and it is through faith we receive the grace that saves us. This is why Christians differ in successfulness in their walk of righteousness. This is most important not to miss because of this fact: Heb 11:6, *But without faith it is impossible to please him: for he that cometh to God must believe that he is, and that he is a rewarder of them that diligently seek him.*

Look, believing God will reward us with our sanctification requires a diligence in seeking that your faith will pursue until acquired! This idea that God will do it all is the formula for failure. Here is what I mean: Peter's faith was initially too weak for sufficient grace to keep him from falling! That is why after his conversion and growth in faith he was able to report to us this truth found in 2Peter 1:5-10, which concludes with the amazing claim that "we *will never fall*". This must be believed in order for it to be attained! Not only attained, but also that God will actually reward your faith with this promised sanctification that diligence of seeking manifests! Otherwise, God does not give the grace for it! This is why the early church discipled inquirers up to three years before baptizing them 'into Christ'. They had to want a sanctified spirit enough to be willing to die for it! The spirit of instant gratification and the false teaching of Calvinism that lays on God the actions required to obtain is blasphemy! Herein lies the ignorance and apathy of our day that hinders not only sanctification, but also Christian Perfection: the mandated responsibility to be holy and the command to be morally perfect is taught to be something God will do: in the meantime we'll teach justification for ongoing transgressions and proclaim that *no mere man can 'perfectly' satisfy the righteous requirements of God's law.* This is FOLLY OF THE CHURCHES and a **'millstone around the neck of its teachers!'**

> *But to say that faith is God's gracious gift, which He maintains, is not to say that faith operates apart from the human will. It is the faith of Christians. They believe. They remain steadfast. They are not passive in the process. The means by which God maintains their faith involves their full participation.*

> *They cannot persevere apart from faith, only through faith.*

First, faith is not a gift as stated above, though all men are given a measure of faith (Rom 12:3). There is a gift of faith that, as other spiritual gifts, are *given severally*, but not to all (Rom 12:6). In Ephesians 2:8 the 'gift' is properly 'grace' that saves and our faith is the conduit through which it comes to us! To teach a sinning-saint is doublespeak. "Steadfast" to what? Being a 'sinning saint'? More subterfuge. The no matter what statement shows their position. Remaining steadfast to a process is different than remaining steadfast to God! (Which is keeping the holy commandment.) It is what transpires before and *brings to completion* the consummation of one event! Obeying His commands, such as to 'sin no more', reveals our belief in Jesus. This is what we are to be *'steadfast'* in, our love for God. This will complete the beginning of our faith, even the salvation of our souls. Jesus will find faith at His return among those who obeyed. Calvinism's Perseverance circumvents the "terms of the Covenant" and sells a false hope.

> *Christians are strengthened by the testing of their faith. "In this you greatly rejoice, even though now for a little while, if necessary, you have been distressed by various trials, that the proof of your faith, being more precious than gold which is perishable, even though tested by fire, may be found to result in praise and glory and honor at the revelation of Jesus Christ" (1Pet 1:5-6). This statement tells the chief means by which God maintains the faith of Christians: He subjects it to trials.*
>
> *The little phrase "you greatly rejoice" may catch the unsuspecting reader off guard. Remember*

the recipients of this epistle were facing life-threatening persecutions. They were fearful of the future. Yet Peter says, "You greatly rejoice." How could they be rejoicing?

Trials produce joy because the testing establishes the faith of Christians. James said exactly the same thing: "Consider it all joy, my brethren, when you encounter various trials, knowing that the testing of your faith produces endurance" (Jas 1:2-3). Temptations (same word as for "trials" in the Greek) and tests do not weaken or shatter real faith just the opposite. They strengthen it. <u>People who lose their faith in a trial only show that they never had real faith to begin with.</u> Real faith emerges from trials stronger than ever.

How can you lose faith that you never had? If it wasn't faith lost, what was lost?

God does not maintain the faith of Christians! We must not only maintain, but also add to, our faith (2Pt 1:5). We are tested to produce patient endurance. Faith can be abandoned; it can be forfeited, it can be lost. Testing also exercises our faith. Faith as a badge that entitles all who claim it to eternal life <u>no matter what</u>, will not acquire grace. Grace has appeared <u>to teach us</u> *"to say no to ungodliness and live righteous,* **holy and upright lives in this present age**,*"* Titus 2:12. Yes, this grace has appeared and is available *"to all people"* Titus 2:11, not just the 'elect.' You see, what they claim faith to be and do, while not true, has become a lie commonly believed. Jesus said, *"Have faith in God!"* This god that Calvinist's are proclaiming will save you, is the iniquitous idol of Perseverance in an unsanctified life; sin never totally departed in the here and now, because their faith denies such a place before the Appearing. Plus, a Calvinist defines the grace, which God meant to empower us through our faith, to be mercy, which diverts God's power from deliverance to a delusional belief of justified active sin! Having then established their faith in a lie, God's grace becomes a covering for sin that is taught to be permanent till the 'last time'.

It is not a faith that produces obedience in holiness, which is obedience to God! The Catechism they revere leaves them in bondage. They also have said in this article that Christians are not perfect here. In other words, no matter how much babble to the contrary, they must maintain their sinning saint status so they won't lose their paycheck. The same reason the Pharisees and the teachers of the law (lawyers) wanted Jesus dead. They didn't want to lose their place and nation, i.e. their livelihood (paycheck). Called hirelings, they minister for money, which they refer to as your tithe. (By the way, something you do not owe as the tithe was part of the Mosaic Law that was nailed to the cross. You remember I said they *'add and take away'* contrary to truth? This is one such case. 'Free will' giving is another matter, but the tithe was an ordinance in Jewish law, (Eph 2:15; Heb 7:12).

> *Trials themselves are anything but joyful, and Peter recognizes this: "though now for a little while, if necessary, you have been distressed by various trials" (v.6). They come like fire to burn the dross off metal. But that is the point. The faith that emerges is that much more glorious. When the fire has done its burning, what is left is <u>purer</u>, brighter, stronger <u>faith</u>.*

FAITH

MacArthur speaks much about faith and its being purified over the course of a believer's life. Again, faith is not something that gets purified, it is an obedience walked in! We all are given a *'measure of faith'*. It does not need to be purified for it is not polluted when God gives it. Faith can increase by hearing the Word of God, but that increase should not be called a groweth in purification of faith. It is an increase of understanding first, and then an action of compliance! For instance, the early church would disciple up to three years those coming into the Church before their baptism. This was done in order to determine the catechumens' faith to truly believe and embrace **"the rule of faith"**, which was 'no sin after baptism.'

Actually, what is said to be left is a purified *soul.* Souls are being saved and purified, not faith. Our faith is being tested. This is a misspeak by Mr. MacArthur. The object of purification is not our faith, but our hearts. We must be *"pure of heart"* (Mat 5:8) *"in order to see God"*, as opposed to pure in faith. *"If I have all faith to…it profits me nothing."* (1Cor 13)

※ ※ ※

CHAPTER TEN

For whom does God test the faith of Christians? For His own sake? Is He wanting to find out whether their faith is real? Of course not. He knows. He tests them for their own benefit, so that they will know if their faith is genuine. He tests their faith in order to refine it, strengthen it, bring it to maturity. What emerges from the crucible is "more precious than gold" (v.7). Unlike gold, proven faith has eternal value. Gold may survive the refiner's fire, but it does not pass the test of eternity. Peter was not giving these Christians empty platitudes. He had tasted the joy that accrues from a trial of persecution. Acts 5:41 says the apostles "went on their way from the presence of the Council [i.e., the Sanhedrin], rejoicing that they had been considered worthy to suffer shame for His name" (emphasis added). They probably went on their way with a stronger faith too. They had suffered, but their faith had passed the test. The great confidence of the believer is to know that his

> *faith is real. Thus trials produce that <u>mature</u> <u>faith</u> by which God preserves Christians.*

The heart and soul of Perseverance is a perfected faith. This diverts the focus from the individual to a substance unseen, which enables the assertion that your 'faith' is what is being purified and not your character that God and men see! This also robs God of His manifold wisdom being seen by principalities and rulers in the heavenly realms. Puts me in mind of the Titanic, it just couldn't sink. Their faith was in an 'unsinkable' ship, which proved to be a false hope; similarly, the Calvinist's false hope is in the ship of Perseverance of the Saints. It will be found to be their titanic unless they are abiding in the terms of the covenant which enable Luke 1:75. Mature faith is another misplaced phrase! Mature is often used in modern translations in place of the word "perfect". Therefore, to say 'a mature faith' diverts true Christian maturity from "moral <u>perfection</u>" to a thing not found in the Word of God!

The point really being made by Calvinists is that your faith will save you. What MacArthur has been implying all along is that if you sin under trial, like Peter's denial, your faith is what guarantees your inheritance. That is, faith in the belief you're saved in spite of ongoing sin proving your faithfulness, (as opposed to your faithfulness under trial being proven by your steadfastness in uprightness)! The revealing of our faith, evidenced by Christian perfection, is what results in *our* honoring God, which brings *Him* praise. This is the revelation of 'Christ in you', the hope of glory. There was no honor or praise for God, let alone for Peter, when Peter swore and denied He knew the Lord. This is 'dressing-up' a lie as truth.

This is why **James** said in **2:14**, *what good is it, my brothers, if someone says he has faith but does not have works? <u>Can that faith save him?</u>* And Paul said in **1Thessalonians**

1:3, *remembering before our God and Father your work of faith and labor of love and steadfastness of hope in our Lord Jesus Christ.* A faith that works is a faith that obeys, which is different than MacArthur's claimed faith that is impure and only partially obeys. The example of this is given to us by God in regard to the children of Israel disobeying His command to go into their **"inheritance"** and take it!

That bunch did not go in because they didn't believe they could defeat their enemy! So, they refused to obey. Because they did not believe God, *"He swore in His wrath they would 'never' enter His rest!"* You must believe that God's grace can give you the victory over every temptation of the enemy of your soul! 1Jn 5:4, *for everyone who has been born of God overcomes the world. And this is the victory that has overcome the world-our faith.* This is not a faith that needs purifying! No, this is a faith that 'overcomes' in the sense of a victory, not by an unknown quantification of certainty in its quality as heretics proclaim! The Old Christian Hymn says, *If you believe, you shall receive. There's not a trouble or care the Good Lord can't relieve!*

* * *

THE ACTIONS OF FAITH REVEALED

So, how does this all fit with the other scriptures referring to these things and Christ's statement to those who protest on Judgment day that they were in fellowship? BEHOLD: The Calvinist is half right about election and predestination. **Rom 8:30**, *Moreover whom he did predestinate, them he also called: and whom he called, them he also justified: and whom he justified, them he also glorified.* Predestinate, called, justified, glorified are all in the past tense! **Act 26:18**, *to open their eyes that they may turn from darkness to light and from the power of Satan unto God, that they may receive* **remission of sins** *and an inheritance among them* *that **are sanctified** by faith in me.* **1Co 6:11** *And such were some of you: but ye are washed, but ye are sanctified, but ye are justified in the name of the Lord Jesus, and by the Spirit of our God.* These verses show the reason that justification and glorification in Romans 8:30 is preceded by being sanctified! The order has been reversed for so long that it makes truth seem to be in error.

What does Jesus say to this thinking? **Luke 13:27-28** *But he shall say, I tell you, I know you not whence ye are; depart from me, all ye workers of iniquity. There shall be weeping and gnashing of teeth, when ye shall see Abraham, and Isaac, and Jacob, and all the prophets, in the kingdom of God, and you yourselves thrust out.* If you understood that to be 'in Christ' is to be out of sin and a 'sanctified believer' is out of sin, and a saint is not a sinner, then you can perceive that *'workers of iniquity'* will not enter the kingdom of God. This most Calvinists and Catholics admit to. What they have perverted is all the scriptures that declare present tense sanctification, which means if you are not out of all known sin now you are 'none of His.'

If they taught this Biblically inspired writ of truth, they would lose a large following! So to serve their own face they do dishonor to the Lord of Glory who sanctified, in eternity past, all who will die to their sin *through faith*, symbolized by a Christian Baptism. **1Cor 1:2,** *"to the assembly of God that is in Corinth, to those sanctified in Christ Jesus, called saints, with all those calling upon the name of our Lord Jesus Christ in every place--both theirs and ours"* And then there is a people that use His name, many of which are church people: *"Not everyone who says to Me Lord Lord shall enter the kingdom of heaven"* (Mat 7:21), which adds, *"only he who does the will of my Father in heaven."* Who does the will of God? 'He who sins no more' is he who is called a saint. People in church that are professing the name of the Lord are no way guaranteed anything, unless they partake of a true Christian baptism, (death to sin with Christ Jesus). Sanctification is not a work of a lifetime as MacArthur and Calvinism suggests it to be. Indeed not, but a present tense dying to the darkness of Satan, which produces the immediate manifestation of the *"remission of sin"*, as it did in Paul.

Heb 10:26-29, *For there is no longer any sacrifice that will take away sins if we purposely go on sinning after the truth has been made fully known to us. Instead, all that is left is to wait in fear for the coming Judgment and the fierce fire which will destroy those who oppose God! Anyone who disobeys the Law of Moses is put to death without any mercy when judged guilty from the evidence of two or more witnesses. What, then, of those who despise the Son of God? Who treat as a cheap thing the blood of God's covenant, which purified them from sin? Who insult the Spirit of grace? Just think how much worse is the punishment they will deserve!*

There was a time the church father Tertullian believed this very thing! Alas, he departed from it, as did the *universal church*. This departure was not as yet a departure from 'no sin after baptism', rather just from the above scripture teaching of *'a full knowledge accompanied with willful sin'*, which terminated your 'guaranteed' salvation. The beast and its image deny it to this day. Those possessing a *full knowledge of the truth* are the same as Hebrews 5:12-14's 'perfect man'. One and the same! These who pollute the blood of God's covenant, *which* purified them from sin, are those who do not maintain their baptism! (1Pt 4:1; 1Jn 5:18) That is, turns back *'like a sow that was washed to wallowing again in the mire'*. This is he who willfully sins after being perfected! That man has no hope of heaven because to do so would be to crucify the Lord afresh and put Him to an open shame! (Heb 6:6) Purified does not mean a covering for willful sin. Under the Law a covering was provided. There is no covering in the Gospel; there is purification under the Gospel, sanctification. What is being taught in our scripture passage in Hebrews 10 is that a 'perfected man' who willfully sins will receive the 'more severe punishment'. This is neither a hypothetical situation nor an idle threat that the unbiblical promise of perseverance negates.

> *Christians are preserved by God for ultimate glory. "The proof of your faith ... may be found to result in praise and glory and honor at the revelation of Jesus Christ" (v.7). Here is an astonishing promise. The ultimate result of proven faith will be praise, glory, and honor at Christ's appearing. The direction of this praise is from God to the believer, not vice versa! Peter is not talking about Christians' praising, glorifying, and honoring God, but His approval directed to them.*
>
> *First Peter 2:20 says, "If when you do what is right and suffer for it you patiently endure it, this finds favor with God." Like the master of the faithful servant, God will say, "Well done, good and faithful slave, . . . enter into the joy of your master" (Matt 25:21). Romans 2:29 says, "He is a Jew who is one inwardly; and circumcision is that which is of the heart, by the Spirit, not by the letter; and his praise is not from men, but from God" (emphasis added). True faith, tested and proved, receives praise from God.*
>
> *Notice 1Pet 1:13 where Peter writes, "Therefore, gird your minds for action, keep sober in spirit, fix your hope completely on the grace to be brought to you at the revelation of Jesus Christ." What is that grace? "Praise and glory and honor." In 4:13 he says, "To the degree that you share the sufferings of Christ, keep*

> *on rejoicing; so that also at the revelation of His glory, you may rejoice with exultation." Paul says, "I consider that the sufferings of this present time are not worthy to be compared with the glory that is to be revealed to us" (Rom 8:18).*
>
> *Some people misunderstand 1Pet 1:7 and think it is saying that faith has to wait for the Second Coming to be found genuine. "That the proof of your faith . . . may be found [worthy] at the revelation of Jesus Christ" as if the outcome were uncertain until that day. But the verse actually says that **faith**, already tested and proved genuine, is **awaiting its eternal reward**. There is no insecurity in this. In fact, the opposite is true. Christians can be certain of the final outcome, because God Himself is preserving them through faith until that day.*

I am amazed that this admission is being made in regards to faith already being proved *at the revelation of Jesus Christ* but, as far as the holiness of the believer, Mr. MacArthur and a whole host of others leave sin intact until Christ appears. If all the claims in regards to Christians sinning for an indeterminate period of time, up to their demise, had not been claimed, then Mr. MacArthur would be in agreement with Justin Martyr, Polycarp, Ignatius, John Chrysostom and the Apostles and our Lord. The Fathers taught a complete cessation of sin. The Apostles commanded it and our Lord based *eternal life* upon it! (Jn 8:31-35)

However, please note in the paragraph above, there is no mention, directly or indirectly, to the sin issue, only to faith and persecution. It is really misleading to talk about faith that is already tested and proved genuine "at the revelation of Jesus Christ", implying, in any sense, faith has been awaiting a final reward! What waits is the creation, for our adoption as sons! MacArthur almost said, by this personalization of faith, that it receives eternal life. Hearing "well done" on Judgment Day is based on the *doing* that comes from an 'obedience of faith'. A diversion to a reward for a job well done, being hidden under the idea of purified faith, turns the *grace of God into an uncontrollable amoral nature!* That is why they keep a final purification until the end.

> *Christians are motivated by love for the Savior. "Though you have not seen Him, you love Him, and though you do not see Him now, but believe in Him, you greatly rejoice with joy inexpressible and full of glory" (v.8). That is a profound statement about the character of genuine faith. Without doubt, two key factors that guarantee perseverance from the human side are love for and trust in the Savior. Peter knew this better than anyone.*

Indeed it is, but love for God cannot really be claimed if sin is not actually STOPPED. John 14:15, *If ye love me, keep my commandments.* 1Peter 1:22, "Now that you have obeyed the truth and have purified your souls to love your brothers sincerely, you must love one another intensely and with a pure heart." Romans 13:10, "Love never does anything that is harmful to its neighbor. Therefore, love is the fulfillment of the law." Obeying the Lord's commandments is *'fulfilling all the laws righteous requirements'*, Romans 8:4, which are met in the act of *love for the brethren* and by *walking in Spirit.* Therefore this, and this alone, is the character of genuine faith. To even suggest a "genuine" faith without entering into *the holy commandment* is surety of rejection on "that Day". "In as much as you have done it unto the least of these, you have done it unto me." (Jesus) That is how we love Jesus, 'doing unto others.' and 'not knowingly violating His commands'.

Here is how Peter described knowing what love and trust is not: *For if, after they have escaped the defilements of the world through the knowledge of our Lord and Savior Jesus Christ, they are again entangled in them and overcome, the last state has become worse for them than the first. For it would have been better for them never to have known the <u>way of righteousness</u> than after knowing it to turn back from <u>the holy commandment</u> delivered to them. What the true proverb says has happened to them: "The dog returns to its own vomit, and the sow, after washing herself, returns to wallow in the mire."* (2Pt 2:20-22)

Please consider: The apostle Peter likened turning from the way/path of righteousness, (which Jesus walked), to a dog returning to its own vomit. The apostle Peter was referring to sin when he likened turning away from righteousness to a dog returning to its own vomit. MacArthur claims Peter knew this faith and trust better than anyone, and he is right; in so far as Peter learned trust and faith being based on faithfulness *to the holy commandment.* Without this, Peter calls us dogs – just as Jesus did when referring to those in Revelation 22:15, *"Without are the dogs, and the sorcerers, and the fornicators, and the murderers, and the idolaters, and <u>everyone</u> that loveth and maketh a lie"*. The Holy Commandment is *"You must be holy for I am a holy I AM!"*

> *After he denied Christ, Peter had to face Jesus Christ and have his love questioned. Jesus asked him three times, "Do you love Me?" and Peter was deeply grieved (John 21:17). Of course, he did love Christ, and that is why he returned to Him and was restored. Peter's own <u>faith was purified by that trial. Peter portrays a beautiful humility</u> here. Peter commends these suffering believers and says to them, "You've*

> *never seen Him and you love Him, and you don't see Him now but you believe in Him." He must have been remembering that when he denied Christ, he was standing close enough for their eyes to meet (Luke 22:60-61). Surely the pain of his own failure was still very real in his heart, after these many years.*
>
> *A normal relationship involves love and trust for someone you can know face-to-face. But Christians love Someone they cannot see, hear, or touch. It is a supernatural, God-given love. "We love him, because he first loved us" (1 John 4:19, KJV).*
>
> *There is no such thing as a Christian who lacks this love*

And that no such thing is a love that obeys that holy commandment! Does not the Peter that we are told knows failure better than any did, also know what must now be obeyed better than today's teachers? Peter's faith was not purified. Peter's faith had more love added to it! John did not deny the Lord; his love was already there.

> *Peter is saying categorically that the essence of what it means to be a Christian is to love Jesus Christ. In fact, perhaps no better way exists to describe the essential expression of the new nature than to say it is continual love for Christ. The King James Version translates 1Pet 2:7 thus: "Unto you therefore which believe he is precious." Note what Paul said in the last verse of Ephesians: "Grace be with all those who love our Lord Jesus Christ with a love incorruptible"(6:24). Paul makes*

> *his strongest statement on this matter in 1Cor 16:22: "If anyone does not love the Lord, <u>let him be accursed</u>.*

<u>Incorruptible love</u> is obedience to *the holy commandment, without which we will be accursed as without holiness no man can see the Lord,* (Heb 12:14). Unfortunately, He said we don't love Him unless we are *"keeping His commandments"*. True faith and love towards God is proved in obedience, *'If you love Me you will obey…'*This is saving faith as opposed to saying, "I believe." (James 2:18-24) And the difference in understanding is their teaching on sin. *Test all things, every spirit.* <u>Let him be accursed</u> is self-applied!

> *Easy-believeism theology ignores this vital truth. Consequently, many people who utterly lack any love for the Lord Jesus Christ are being given a false hope of heaven.*

INDEED.

> *True Christians love Christ. His love for them, producing their love for Him (1John 4:19), is one of the <u>guarantees that they will persevere to the end</u> (Rom 8:33 -39). Jesus said, "If you love Me, you will keep My commandments" (John 14:23). "He who has My commandments and keeps them, <u>he it is who loves Me</u>" (John 14:21). Conversely, "He who does not love Me does not keep My words" (John 14:24).*

SEPARATION FROM GOD'S LOVE

Let's get something straight here! To say you believe there is no perfection here for Christians, (stated earlier by MacArthur), and then quote John 14:21 is to silently say,

'You will not, however, be able to love Him perfectly while in the flesh'. I ask those who think Calvinism really does teach 'you have to be holy to get into God's kingdom', do you see a problem with not keeping Jesus' *holy commandment* fully and then suggesting that is still love for the Lord? Can you see the FOLLY in that? Or do you like the Calvinistic slant of an imperfect Christian who will only partially 'obey' Jesus and say they are loving God? If you are a Calvinist that may be why you are. A little license eliminates the mandate of a *holy presentation of your body,* which Paul defined as your *"reasonable"* worship (Rom 12:1-2). Calvinism provides an 'unreasonable' worship of sin every day and according to them it is still *"love for God".* (What's more, it *guarantees* they will persevere to the end.) And then they present Romans 8:33-39 in a false light, as if it says *nothing* will prevent our eternal security is just plain deceptive. Here is love for God: John 14:21, 15:10; 1John 5:2, 3; 2John 1:6.

The context of Romans 8:33-39 includes verses 29-32! Why? Because the *promise of nothing separating us from GOD'S LOVE, or being able to condemn us,* all hangs on verse 29; *"conformity to the image of God's Son",* (just as in Luke 1:75), here on planet earth. Without that we are open to being a *transgressor and a vile person,* as Saul was *before he became Paul.* If, like him, we find mercy for our *ignorance* then, and only then, upon our real repentance will we be able to be conformed to His image. And that not 'imperfectly', as Calvinism and MacArthur teach, trying to deceive you with their *perversion of the Word,* as they do throughout the Epistle of Romans. Ask yourself this: do you believe holiness means less than sinlessness? Do you think *'sin no more'* means 'sin less'? Do you believe *'now that you have been set free from sin'* means just its consequences? If you could not say a resounding NO, you're conforming to Calvinism and are greatly deceived. Deceived as in Ezekiel 14:4 and 2Thessalonians 2:10-12. Walk in those opinions and you will *perish in them.*

Those who are devoted to Christ long to promote His glory. They long to serve Him with heart and soul and mind and strength. They delight in His beauty. They love to talk about Him, read about Him, fellowship with Him. They desire to know Him better and to know Him deeper. They are compelled in their hearts to want to be like Him. Like Peter, they may stumble frequently and fail in pathetic ways as sinful flesh assaults holy longings. But like Peter, all true believers will persevere until the goal is ultimately reached. "Beloved, now we are the children of God, and it has not appeared as yet what we shall be. We know that, when He appears, we shall be like Him, because we shall see Him just as He is" (1John 3:2).

1 John 3:2 is speaking of the glorification a saint 'will' experience at the last day (His appearing). Remember if you claim to be in Christ *"...He appeared to take away sins, and in Him there is no sin"*, John 3:5. This appearance to take away sins is not a reference to Jesus Second Coming! *Remission* was provided for during His first appearance! Have you availed yourself of this grace, His power to take you out of sin?

"So that, as sin reigned in death, **grace also might reign through righteousness** *leading to eternal life through Jesus Christ our Lord"* (Rom 5:21).

IF we have holy longings we will be filled with their fruit long before Christ's next appearing. Jesus taught *"he that hungers after righteousness shall be filled"*, Matthew 5:6. And no, this cannot be referring to Second Advent because the result of obeying these things is 5:48 NKJV: *"therefore you will be perfect as your Father in heaven is perfect!"* What follows a holy longing after righteousness is being filled with righteousness, Biblical Christian perfection in the here and now! MacArthur and Calvinism substitute this moral perfection for a personal affirmation that "sin is a reality in the believer's experience, so it is clear that insistence on the Slavic necessity of a working faith does not include the idea of perfectionism."

The Serpent's ministers may appear as ministers of righteousness, but inside are ravenous wolves! It is Peter who said that very thing. You know, that apostle that John MacArthur says you will be following in failure in spite of 'holy longings'? And, also like Peter, will not reach that ultimate goal until Christ's appearing. This lie is two-fold: 1) insisting even the apostles were all still sinners till seeing Christ a second time; 2) the promotion of your 'personal affirmation', which is what they are selling and their communicants are buying. This is the merchandising of the *"souls of men"*, (Rev 18:13). 'Come out of her God's people.'

> *Leighton, writing in 1853 in a wonderful commentary on 1Peter, said this:*
>
> *Believe, and you shall love; believe much, and you shall love much; labor for strong and deep persuasion of the glorious things which are spoken of Christ, and this will command love. Certainly, did men indeed believe his worth, they would accordingly love him; for the reasonable creature cannot but affect that most which it firmly believes to be the worthiest of affection. Oh! this mischievous unbelief is that which makes the heart cold and dead towards God. Seek then to believe Christ's excellency in himself and his love to us, and our interest in him, and this will kindle such a fire in the heart, as will make it ascend in a sacrifice of love to him.*

An important point needs to be made from the statement "believe much, and you shall love much". Jesus said *'he who is forgiven much will love much'*, Luke 7:47. "Faith comes by hearing the Words of God", Romans 10:17, but love for the Lord comes from being forgiven our wrongs and Peter was forgiven much, even as Paul, therefore they loved much. They believed much because they heard much, as the Lord personally taught them, even as you and I can be taught, when we sit at Jesus' feet, for He said in John 5:39-40;

"You search the Scriptures because you think that in them you have eternal life; and it is they that bear witness about me, yet you refuse to come to me that you may have life."

I wrote this book reader, to direct you to what Jesus taught with the hope you will go to *Him*. Men can go to the scriptures and then teach from them, but without sitting at Jesus' feet and learning from Him, they may well be just teaching their own mind on a given matter. If you go to Him your faith will increase in the Truth himself.

> *So love for Christ is another of the means God uses to assure our perseverance. That love and the faith that accompanies it are a source of inexpressible joy, full of glory (1Pet 1:8).*
>
> *Christians are saved by a working faith. "[You are] obtaining as the outcome of your faith the salvation of your souls" (1:9). In this phrase Peter speaks of a present deliverance. "Obtaining" is a present-tense verb, middle voice. The word could be literally translated, "Presently receiving for yourselves . . ." This present salvation is "the outcome" of a Christian's faith a working faith. In* **practical terms**, *it means a present-tense deliverance* **from** *sin, guilt, condemnation, wrath, ignorance, distress, confusion, hopelessness*

> *'everything that defiles'. This does not speak of the future perfect consummation of salvation mentioned in v. 5.*

Everything that defiles. This claim was covered in chapter seven, and stated there *not* to mean 'sinlessness' until the end. Restated here as follows: The phrase, "a salvation ready to be revealed in the last time," speaks of full and final salvation [sic] the curse of the law, the power and presence of sin. The old adage *"figures don't lie, but liars figure"* is never truer than the comparison above reveals, where now he says it does 'mean a present-tense deliverance from sin'. Unlike in chapter 7, he's telling the truth, i.e., the verse does teach a present-tense deliverance from sin!

So why doesn't a Calvinist just come out and plainly say they mean, 'even though the deliverance is available, it is not attainable till the end'? If they did, it would become too obvious a denial of the affirmation just given of present-tense deliverance and, since they are not selling present-tense deliverance from sin, they claim it only happens in v. 5. Perfect is not mentioned in verse five, consummation or otherwise. It is speaking of being able to see, through the eyes of faith, the salvation to be revealed in the last time, eternal life imparted. Not seeing our salvation *perfected* in the last time, but seeing the inheritance, which is being kept in heaven, incorruptible, become ours. Predicated all along on being in God's power (grace), which our faith keeps us supplied with.

Now you can see again how they define present-tense deliverance from sin, they never actually mean *'deliverance'* from all sinful acts, i.e., experiential holiness! Deliverance does not mean that to them. They reserve it for 1Peter 1:5, which to MacArthur is kept to be finished *'in the last time'*. But I proclaim to all who can hear, faith in a lie will not make that lie truth. 'Future perfect consummation' is their way of covering up their loved doctrine of 'faith in imperfection brings the consummation of heaven'. Anathema, says the Apostle to them who preach another gospel, (Gal 1:8). Their gospel is not the Gospel that *delivers from all unrighteousness* in the here and now, therefore the apostles' curse will be theirs. Sanctimonious Churchianity, even with *feigned piety*, which rejects the holy commandment, is called false humility.

"These things look like wisdom with their self-imposed worship, false humility, and harsh treatment of the body. But they have no value for holding back the constant desires of your corrupt nature", (Col 2:23.)

> *The salvation in view in v.9 is a constant, present-tense salvation. Sin no longer has dominion over Christians (Rom 6:14). They can in no way fail to persevere. They will certainly fail at times and will not always be successful. In fact, some people may seem to experience more failure than success.* But no true believer can fall into settled unbelief or permanent reprobation. To allow for such a possibility is a disastrous misunderstanding of God's keeping power in the lives of His chosen ones.

The underlined portion above confirms my claim that "present-tense deliverance" never really means *'free from sin'* to a Calvinist or MacArthur or most Evangelicals. And as shown later, Protestants just mirror Catholicism in this matter. This 'matter' amounts to the 'core of the Gospel', and thusly, like a beast without understanding, they have wandered away from the truth! If *present tense* deliverance from sin is true, then Christ really did provide deliverance to the uttermost, and it is incumbent upon us to *make every effort to be found in Him without any spot or wrinkle, which makes our calling and election sure.* But Mr. MacArthur has provided license from the very beginning of his discourse. Again, given enough time and space, that which is repeatedly stated becomes common knowledge, but *is revealed to be one of their common lies.*

Until their Carnal Tent of Faith - saints are sinners - is dealt with they cannot be *"without spot or wrinkle at His appearing"*, because sin is a spot and He's coming back for a spotless bride. He is not coming back to *make* her spotless, but to *pick* her *up* spotless (Jam 1:27). Theirs is a *'strange doctrine'*, not in the Word or in the early Church, but 'common knowledge' in the modern churches. So, is the sinning believer saved no matter what? Plus, their claim of no permanent reprobation shows my assertion that they mean you cannot die while in sin. Can you still hang your hat on those lies?

> *Thus Peter opens his first epistle. At the end of this same epistle he returns to the theme of perseverance: "After you have suffered for a little while, the God of all grace, who called you to His eternal glory in Christ, will Himself perfect, confirm, strengthen and establish you" (5:10).*

> *The magnitude of that promise is overwhelming! God Himself perfects, confirms, strengthens, and establishes His children. Though His purposes for the future involve some pain in the present, He will nevertheless give Christians grace to endure and persevere. Even while they are being personally attacked by the enemy, they are being personally perfected by God. He Himself is doing it. He will accomplish His purposes in them, bringing them to wholeness, setting them on solid ground, making them strong, and*

> *establishing them on a firm foundation. All those terms speak of strength and resoluteness.*

It must be remembered this is after you have suffered for doing good, not evil (1Pt 4:16)! Silence concerning evil being a possible cause of a Christian's suffering is very dangerous for a struggling believer. 'Resist the devil and he will flee.' (James)

"If you suffer, it must *not be because you are a murderer or a thief or a criminal or a meddler in other people's affairs"* (1Pt 4:15).

It is this kind of selective teaching that leaves the unlearned in darkness. Paul informed the Ephesian elders he was *'free from the blood of all men'* because *'he proclaimed the* **whole** *council of God'* to them. Acts 20:26-28. This kind of silence on the sin issue does not betoken consent, but is an evidence of deception and acceptance. Quantification of sin being left an uncertain commodity leaves room for license, and that is exactly what they are doing. The word "must" in the verse above is an imperative, and being so, addresses the false claim by Ryrie and MacArthur of the uncertain quantification below.

※ ※ ※

CHAPTER ELEVEN

THE PROBLEM OF QUANTIFICATION

Inevitably, the question is raised, "How faithfully must one persevere?" Ryrie has written,
> *So we read a statement like this: "A moment of failure does not invalidate a disciple's credentials." My immediate reaction to such a statement is to want to ask if two moments would? Or a week of defection, or a month, or a year? Or two? How serious a failure and for how long before we must conclude that such a person was in fact not saved? Lordship teaching recognizes that "no one will obey perfectly," but the crucial question is simply how imperfectly can one obey and yet be sure that he "believed"?*

This is designer Christianity! These questions posed by our Calvinist heretics are all based on the presupposed belief that Christian Perfection does not exist. The presenting of a false premise, namely: "how imperfectly can one obey", is a question designed to elicit the idea disobedience is acceptable behavior in a Christian. Example: a father tells his son to go to school and bring his homework home after school and have it done by the time he arrives in the evening. The boy goes to school, brings home *some* of his homework and then goes out to play. Has the boy obeyed his father? The truth is he simply 'disobeyed'! Quantification is irrelevant!

What Ryrie and MacArthur want you to think is, since the boy 'partially obeyed' he still can continue to believe his disobedience is acceptable. It is adding to the Word of God! There is no such thing as imperfect obedience, you either obey or you don't. In fact, they want you to think your life long character will be disobedience! Thus they teach in their catechism we sin everyday in word, though and deed. They call it a Christian catechism, but the first Christian catechism, called the Didaché, taught directly opposite, as does the Word of God.

The children of Israel obeyed and left Egypt, they obeyed Moses, as God's oracle giver, by going through the Red Sea, but they did not obey and enter Canaan. This quantifiable singular disobedience disqualified them from receiving their promise! This example is given to us to fear God, lest the promise to 'inherit' is negated due to our own disobedience (Heb 4:1-3)! This chapter in Hebrews stresses the permanency of obedience by calling it TODAY (vs7). Therefore, it is incumbent upon us to obey everyday, which is how the Word defines believing. This means able to obey/fulfill today all God's *'righteous requirements'* (Rom 8:4.) This is saved to the uttermost: *to the extreme; to the maximum.* 'Acceptable imperfect obedience' is the invention of heretics. What can be true however is prior to our perfection when we are able to "fully discern good from evil", Hebrews 5:12-14, sins of ignorance may be manifest in a believer's life. Once these sins become known, (as they will by abiding in the light), the disciple must forsake them once for all (1Jn 1:9, 2:6, 3:8). Was it not MacArthur's sinning champion, Peter, who said, ".If you do these things you will never fall!" Yes, quantification is not a mystery after all. 1Peter 4:1 quantifies the amount of sin acceptable!

> *. . . A moment of defection, we have been told, is not an invalidation. Or "the true disciple will never turn away completely." Could he turn away almost completely? Or ninety percent? Or fifty percent and still be sure he was saved?*
>
> *Frankly, all this relativity would leave me in confusion and uncertainty. Every defection, especially if it continued, would make me unsure of my salvation. Any serious sin or unwillingness would do the same. If I come to a fork in the road of my Christian experience and choose the wrong branch and continue on it, does that mean I was never on the Christian road to begin with? For how long can I be fruitless without having a <u>lordship advocate</u> conclude that I was never <u>really saved</u>?*

By their fruit you will know them. Luke 6:43 plainly states, *"For no good tree bears bad fruit, nor again does a bad tree bear good fruit."* That is why Jesus told His disciples to recognize another disciple *'by their fruit'*. What's amazing here is that Ryrie disparagingly faults a <u>lordship advocate</u> for asking, 'Where's the fruit?' As has been repeatedly said by this author, Calvinists really despise Jesus' teachings! And to do so is to be an idolater. How so? Promoting your own teaching over that of the Lord's is making yourself God! All liars will be where? Idolaters where?

> *Ryrie suggests that if we cannot state precisely how much failure is possible for a Christian, true assurance becomes impossible. He wants the terms to be quantified: "Could he turn away almost completely? Or ninety percent? Or fifty percent?" To put it another way, Ryrie is suggesting that the doctrines of perseverance and assurance are incompatible. Astonishingly, he wants a doctrine of assurance that allows those who have defected from Christ to be confident of their salvation.*

And so does MacArthur! He just makes the parameters more obscure!

> *No quantifiable answers to the questions Ryrie raises are available. Indeed, some Christians persist in sin for extended periods of time. But those who do forfeit their right to genuine assurance.*

Neither Ryrie nor McArthur's gospels provide genuine assurance *in truth*, because neither state the assurance has to be according to a quantifiable obedience in order to be genuine. STOP means the acts of sinning cease to happen. They are not taught that if they die in a state of sin they will be damned, because that would be to annul their Security and Perseverance. Therefore it is claimed these questions cannot be answered. Really, the WORD of GOD HIMSELF has answered them in the scriptures and so, if you think you have faith believe Him (Ezk 18:25-27).

> *"Serious sin or unwillingness" certainly should cause someone to contemplate carefully the question of whether he or she really loves the Lord. Those who turn away completely*

> *(not almost completely, or ninety percent, or fifty percent) demonstrate that they never had true faith.*

The underlined above suggests MacArthur is confused here! How can you turn away from what you never had in the first place? Unserious sin is not cause for contemplation? (MacArthur just creates more uncertainties.) Those that turn away, as in Hebrews 6:4, are apostates and, yes, they had all the qualifications of any believer yet chose to turn back, (as Paul reported of Demas, etc.) Their twisted teaching is contrary to the Gospel for this reason: the good news teaches deliverance through the r*emission of sins.* Calvinism teaches a forgiveness only, without the remission of all active sin, directly contradicting Luke 1:75 and Romans 8:2. Hebrews 10:26-29 denotes a true Christian having all that our Covenant offers, even unto a *"full knowledge"* of the truth. IF that one *willfully* sins - and this word declares he can as well as may not - *"there is no more sacrifice"*, that is, no more forgiveness or mercy! Modern Christendom does not tolerate this teaching, however it is God's Word, at least to some of us. Faith indeed. Their faith is in security, saved from hell no matter what. Now it is easier to understand why the early disciples did what they did in Acts 2:40-47. Read it and see.

> *Quantification poses a dilemma for merely-intellectual-faith teaching too. Hodges speaks of faith as a "historical moment." How brief may that moment be? Someone listening to a debate between a Christian and an atheist might believe for an instant while the Christian is speaking, but immediately be led back into doubt or agnosticism by the atheist's arguments. Would such a person be classified as a believer? One suspects some*

> *easy-believeism advocates would answer yes, although that view goes against everything God's word teaches about faith.*
>
> *Jesus never quantified the terms of salvation; He always made them <u>absolute</u>.*

You mean like in <u>no matter what</u>? Which is now, <u>absolute</u>? More double speak!

> "So therefore, no one of you can be My disciple who does not give up all his own possessions" (Luke 14:33);

How about the possession of sin in a believer? False gospel? Freedom rests on truth!

> "He who loves father or mother more than Me is not worthy of Me; and he who loves son or daughter more than Me is not worthy of Me" (Matt 10:37); "He who loves his life loses it; and he who hates his life in this world shall keep it to life eternal" (John 12:25). Those conditions are <u>impossible in human terms</u> (Matt 19:26.)

But mandatory! *'To save our souls we must give up our souls.'* The priority to starting is denying self any liberty to sin! Has Jesus secured deliverance for us in this world? Is present-tense deliverance a partial deliverance? Deliverance is the act of rescuing or setting free, in this case from sin. J. MacArthur just said, in so many words, it is impossible in human terms. True enough! That is why Jesus is our Savior, not ourselves. He brings us God's grace that empowers us to obey the gospel. Believing "it is Jesus that saves us" requires us to give over our life to His will! This is dying to one's own soul in order for it to be saved. So, dying to the 'old man' is what makes us a saint.

Are you willing to forfeit your soul in order to save it? If you are and seal it in the waters of baptism, rising to a *"newness of life"* that comes from putting the *"old man"* to death, you will live! Then you will be a Christian! There is no other kind! Nor is there any other way of putting your *'sins in remission'*. John 8:34-36 plainly states a servant of sin, (one who commits sin, singular here in the Greek,) cannot remain in the 'house' (kingdom of God) forever. That servant who is in bondage must be made 'free indeed'. 'Free indeed' is 'uttermost deliverance' from the acts and power of sin, period! You must forfeit your perceived right to sin. That is the beginning of how to lose your soul so that you may find it.

> *That does not alter or mitigate the truth of the gospel. It certainly is no excuse for going to the other extreme and doing away with <u>any necessity for commitment to Christ.</u>*

It is very possible, as Jesus' teaches, "with God all things are possible". Therefore, whatever is commanded is also provided for, even if the way is straight and the door is narrow. I did not say it was easy, only that His yoke is easier than your burden and bondage of sin and His burden lighter than your cares and burdens of this life.

> *Ryrie's comments raise another issue that is worth considering. It is the question of whether working-faith teaching is inherently judgmental: "How long can I be fruitless without having a lordship advocate conclude that I was never really saved?" Hodges has made a similar comment: "Lordship teaching reserves*

> *to itself the right to strip professing Christians of their claims to faith and to consign such people to the ranks of the lost."*

You mean like in Luke 12:46 or Acts 8:20 or Galatians 1:8? Now, in order to perpetuate his teaching, MacArthur runs back to the famous *politically correct* interpretation of Romans 14:4 & James 4:11. The context of Romans 14:4 is twofold and begins at verse one and ends around verse fourteen. Verse four only defines finding fault with those who worship on a different day and concerning the eating of meat. It is deceptive to ignore those facts and it is adding to the words of God. Now in James 4:11 the word 'judge' is Strong's #2919 and it means *to distinguish, that is, decide* (mentally or judicially); by implication to *try, condemn, punish*.

As stated before, the implication is not to condemn, which is what Paul was pointing out in Romans 14:4; *it is before God we stand or fall*. Paul was commanding the individual believers doing the condemning, and he was making a personal judgment, which is an example to us. Let this sink into your spirit, "judge not that you be not judged" in no way suggests God's people are not to make a "righteous" judgment, which is accomplished by 'removing the beam from our eye first so that we may see clearly to remove the speck from our brothers eye' (Jn 7:24; Rom 2:5). Condemnation is of the Lord, but judgment is given to the saints (1Cor 6:3). The truth shall set free.

> *Certainly <u>no individual</u> can judge another's heart. It is one thing to challenge people to examine themselves (2 Cor 13:5); it is entirely another matter to set oneself up as another Christian's judge (Rom 14:4, 13; Jas 4:11). But though <u>individual Christians must never be judgmental</u>*

But to try and test heretics, is good. (Rev 2:2 and Titus 3:10-11) Unlike in the case of Jim Bakker who said, "We don't say anything negative around here!" The admonition to not judge carries with it the idea *'of not condemning'*. What most church people mean when they say, 'I don't judge' or 'You shouldn't judge', is 'Don't judge me'! This is especially true if you expose heresy, by which someone appears to be in a sin or error, which they cannot disprove or defend. (Denial is not a defense, it is just more sin.) "From the abundance of the heart the mouth speaks."

> *the church body as a whole very definitely has a responsibility to maintain purity by exposing and excommunicating those who live in continual sin or defection from the faith.*

Yes, and this requires making a judgment, as in 1Corinthians 6. It also begins with individual differences between the *brethren*. It requires taking a matter before the whole church only if **one**, *two or three* cannot resolve the issue. That individual Christians must never be judgmental is another misleading statement. While it is true we shouldn't be *judgmental*, it is also true that at times we must make judgments. In fact, we are told to do so, in a righteous manner *"for with the same judgment we use it shall be used unto us"*. This makes a 'righteous judgment' most beneficial to all. Concerning *my* judgment that Calvinism teaches a heresy that promotes sin, consider the Lord's condemnation at this juncture. (Read Mat 13:37-41 and 18:6.)

> The Lord gave very explicit instructions on how to handle a fellow believer who falls into such sin. Christians are to go to the brother (or sister) privately first (Matt 18:15). If he or she refuses to hear, they are to go again with one or two

> more people (Matt 18:16). Then if he or
> she refuses to hear, they are to "tell it
> to the church" (Matt 18:17). If the <u>one
> sinning still fails to repent, "let him be
> to you as a Gentile and a tax-gatherer"</u>
> (Matt 18:17). In other words, pursue that
> person for Christ evangelistically as if he
> or she were utterly unsaved.

And if <u>the one sinning still fails to repent?</u> From this very statement by MacArthur it becomes plain that other sinning brethren, (but of lesser degree), are allowed to judge! What this whole thing proves again is that there really is and must be sanctified present-tense born-again people in the church to make a righteous judgment! *(Let him without sin cast the first stone,* said Jesus.) So by this am I to assume the non-sinning brothers really are the true Christians after all? Look, of course we are all capable of falling into sin, even gross sin, but that is not to say sin is, '<u>to a greater or lesser degree</u>', the norm for any in Christ as <u>MacArthur may have been</u> suggesting by the parade of Peter's sins being inferred to remain a lifetime! On the contrary, this from an apostle:

"*Let not a hint of sexual immorality and all impureness or greediness must not even once be named among you, according as is appropriate for* holy ones *(saints). Neither obscenity, buffoonery, witticisms, these not being suitable, but contrary to graciousness.*" (Eph 5:3-6)

Yes, *holy ones.* Have you been set free from sin? Have you purified yourself by obeying the truth? (1Pt 1:22, 4:1; 2Jn 1:4) A holy one is a saint. The saints will be the judge of the world and angels, not sinners.

> *This process of discipline is how Christ mediates His rule in the church. He added, "Truly*

I say to you, whatever you shall bind on earth shall be bound in heaven; and whatever you loose on earth shall be loosed in heaven. Again I say to you, that if two of you agree on earth about anything that they may ask, it shall be done for them by My Father who is in heaven" (Matt 18:18 -19). The context shows this is not talking about "binding Satan" or about praying in general. The Lord was dealing with the matter of sin and forgiveness among Christians (cf. Matt 18:21 ff.) The verb tenses in v.18 literally mean, "Whatever you bind on earth shall have been bound in heaven; and whatever you loose on earth shall have been loosed in heaven." The Lord said that He Himself works personally in the discipline process: "For where two or three have gathered together in My name, there I am in their midst" (Matt 18:20).

Thus the process of church discipline, properly followed, answers all of Ryrie's questions. How long can a person continue in sin before fellow Christians "conclude that [he or she] was never really saved?" All the way through the discipline process. Once the matter has been told to the church, if the person still refuses to repent, Christians have instructions from the Lord Himself to regard the sinning one "as a Gentile and a tax-gatherer."

The church discipline process outlined in Matthew 18 is predicated on the doctrine of perseverance. Those who remain **hardened in sin** *only demonstrate their lack of true faith.*

How about those **'soft in sin'** like the Catechism teaches? Do they have true faith if they sin every day in word, thought and deed? Are they advocating that daily sin committed by them, those three ways, does not harden them to sin? So what we have in Calvinism is the church agreeing to determine the quantification of serious sin - that 'can't be quantified' – and becoming the accuser and jury of one of the other sinners! This suggests that only so-called *serious* sin needs to be repented of! Their secret, or public sins of a *non*-serious nature, (apparently like Peter's), are ignored and considered to be the everyday sins of 'the prevalency of corruption remaining in them', thereby not requiring final and complete repentance! Because of this, Calvinism teaches the sinning-saint oxymoron.

Concerning the prevalency of corruption remaining in those MacArthur calls saints, you need to know this: as long as that corruption, known as the sin nature, remains in a disciple, he or she can never have a pure heart. Jesus taught **'without a pure heart we cannot see God'**. Romans 6 teaches this sin nature to be rendered dead by the stated 'reckoning' of faith! If you do not exercise your faith to the reality of present-tense sanctification you will never be able to acquire a pure heart! But if you do, by the consecration of yourself to holy things, and you seal it in the waters of purification by the Word Himself, you will be saved unto the uttermost. Not like the Perseverance of the Sinning-Saint heresy that leaves you in sin, defiled until Christ's appearing.

The soul that sinneth still dies! God's gift of eternal life is to those who are experientially holy. If you 'entrust' your fallen nature unto God against "that day" it will be kept as you present it, unholy! Rev 22:11 *He that is unjust, let him be unjust still: and he which is filthy, let him be filthy still: and he that is righteous, let him be righteous still: and he that is holy, let him be holy still.* Present (Rom 12:1-2) yourself "holy" as a reasonable "worship" and He will guard it so, by His power, through your faith (Rom 4:13; Col 2:12)! We are given this power to become God's children when we believe *into* Him (Jn 1:12). The Word of God teaches present-tense holiness as sainthood.

> *Those who respond to the rebuke and return to the Lord give the best possible evidence of genuine salvation. They can be sure that if their faith is real, it will endure to the end because God Himself guarantees it. "I am confident of this very thing, that He who began a good work in you will perfect it until the day of Christ Jesus" (Phil 1:6). "I know whom I have believed and I am convinced that He is able to guard what I have entrusted to Him until that day" (2Tim 1:12).*
>
> *Added to Bible Bulletin Board's "McArthur's Collection":* **END**

* * *

CHAPTER TWELVE

In conclusion, the Westminster Catechism states a Christian *'sins every day three ways'* and also states *'no mere man can perfectly obey the commandments of God!'* Observe how this contradicts Scripture. 1) It suggests the first word of the gospel, repent, can be but imperfectly met. 2) It maligns the meaning of *"being set free from sin"*, (and thereby *"being free indeed"*), to suggest a state that we only arrive at *"in the last time."*

This continues the Roman Catholic Church's Folly, established in 431 A.D., which annulled the previous five centuries' teaching of *"no sin after baptism"*. The Apostle Peter stated, in his discourse on baptism, *"he that has suffered in the flesh has ceased from sin"*. Baptism is the outward confession of *"dying with Christ to sin"*, (Col 2:11-12; Rom 6:1-7), which is *"the answer of a good conscience towards God"*. The flesh, i.e. the 'fallen nature', is made to suffer in ceasing from sin. The fleshly desires die reluctantly and we are told to *"flee the passions of youth"*. Consecration to holy things accomplishes our sanctification by *'the answer of a good conscience'* that says "because I love the Lord, I will not fail to obey Him in all that I know". Even today, will I *'lay aside the sin that so easily besets me'*?

Mr. MacArthur seemed to only have referenced the Catechism when it suited his purposes. However, to align oneself with it is to confirm its contents, unless a disclaimer is stated. MacArthur, the Catechism and Calvinists believe and promote the 'sinning saint' gospel that is so widely **worshipped** today. Their "gospel' is an image of the Beast, invented by an unrepentant murderer, John Calvin.

Deception has had a good two thousand years to infect the apostles' gospel received from the Lord Himself. When the Apostle Paul said, *"I know that as soon as I am gone ravenous wolves would come in, even amongst yourselves, to deceive the flock".* He never added that somewhere down the pike deception would straighten itself out in some kind of reformation. As a matter of fact, none of the other apostles or the Lord Himself hinted at it. What He did suggest was the opposite. *"Will I find faith when I return?"* (A faith that obeys the Law of Christ, as the writer of Hebrews recorded in 5:9).

THE SPIRIT OF ABSOLUTION

Having attended numerous denominations to the point of full familiarity, the Spirit of Christ has made known to me *"the spirit of the age."*

If the Covenant people were so deceived with error and tradition in their day of visitation, is it not likely that the people of this nation, many professing to be Christian, are also deceived in this day and time? This is not some rare phenomenon that only happens to pagans; it is most prevalent among those that profess they are religious and Christian—even as the Jews confessing to be Abraham's children and followers of Moses.

Peter refers to those who have forgotten they were washed from their *"past"* sins. Why does he say this? Are we not all *'sinners* saved by grace'? This phrase is used to suggest God's grace is to leave us in our sin and still "save" us, in the end, from its power and consequence. This is an example of today's deception, which is what 99% of American Protestant Christendom believes today. (And their Catholic counterpart behaves much the same.) Everybody knows thirty thousand sectarians can't be wrong, right?

How has **grace** become the vehicle that takes a Protestant, who claims to be a *sinning* saint, to heaven? Easy. Change the definition of grace to mercy! Admittedly, most of us in our life have needed a double dose of mercy, however this does not justify making grace and mercy synonyms; they are two different things. GRACE is God's power to *"save unto the uttermost" "from every act that leads to death"* (Heb 9:14 NIV). God's MERCY, being part of his character, is why He brought grace through Jesus Christ to man. Not to leave us in sin, but to deliver us *'away from it'* through *the remission of sin.* Mercy is a personality trait of the Almighty, but so is justice and retribution! *Tribulation and anguish, upon every soul of man that doeth evil,* (Rom 2:9). The Law was through Moses, but Grace and Truth are through Jesus Christ. The Law was given to reveal sin. Jesus gave himself and so grace is made available to be appropriated through our faith. As we receive that grace (power) of God that saves **from** sin unto eternal life, we must walk in it!

So having, over the course of time, removed the mandatory provision and condition that was to be entered into – namely, becoming *dead to sin, signified by a public baptism* - we are now told we are sinning saints or, at the very least, saved even if we 'are in known sin when the Lord returns'. (Very well known radio and TV personalities, and many others, teach this false salvation on the Protestant side; the Catholic side provides Purgatory.) It is said, by the many, "all our sins - past, present and future - are already forgiven, all we have to do is confess them". This lie changes being *"dead"* in our trespasses and sins, to being alive in them and destroys true Christian Baptism.

The devil and his ministers having accomplished this *damnable heresy*, we now need a double dose of **mercy** in the Evangelical Camps. In the Orthodox Camps absolution was developed. A century after the teaching of *'no sin after baptism'* was dropped Purgatory was added. Then, during and after the so-called Reformation, the teaching of Perseverance and Once-Saved-Al-ways-Saved, (also referred to as Eternal Security), was brought in. *'He that lives for pleasure is dead, even while he lives'* and so the need for assurances of all types!

"A little leaven leavens the whole lump" and that is exactly what has happened in the modern churches. Beware that the Serpent does not beguile you as he did Eve. Apostasy is not leaving the church, but it is leaving the truth! I encourage you to reach out until you avail yourself of the grace of God found in the Gospel. It is the **power** of God unto salvation, (Rom 1:16), from sin.

Others have the same ability to change a truth by suppressing it with disinformation. Case in point: the United States was, (and according to its Supreme Law still is), a Republic. Beginning in the late sixties and early seventies politicians began to call it a Democracy. It didn't take long before this stuck. Similarly, concepts and whole doctrines have been redefined the past two thousand years, which show the truth of the saying "a thing often repeated becomes common knowledge". So don't marvel at this or that your gospel, in many cases, has been turned into license to sin. I can assure you that Christianity in its virgin form has no equal today. May you seek the Lord's confirmation of the claims I have made in this book and start your journey back to your future. The Truth will set you free from sin, why not go after Him with all your heart, mind, soul and strength?

If you have now believed the apostles' gospel and would be found in Him blameless, undefiled and holy, *which is your reasonable worship,* you will need to have daily alertness and extreme vigilance. *"With great difficulty we shall enter the kingdom of heaven."* Why? Because *"the Way is straight and narrow and few there be who find it"*. You see it really does take consecration. Some might imagine consecration is for a cleric or priest only, however, to be a true Christian IS to be a priest. Priests, like Levi, *"revered God and turned many away from iniquity"*. This requires the consecration spoken of in Romans 12:1-2. To be Jesus' disciple we *"must depart all iniquity"* 2Timothy 2:19. Eternal vigilance is the price of liberty. It is also the price of *"freedom from sin"*, which is the liberty Jesus offers! He is the *"author of eternal salvation to those who obey Him"*. Let no one deceive you, *"whatsoever a person sows that shall he also reap"*. The Lord is kind and compassionate to all He has made. Reach out He is waiting for you.

Enquiries can be made by contacting:
00jpalmer@gmail.com

Books can be purchased from Amazon at $6.03 USD.